D0467299

Shannon Huffman Polson has written a soulful and brave book about death, life, and the complexities surrounding both. There is nothing sentimental in these pages. *North of Hope* shows us how personal loss and loss of our planet come from the same place: Love. This is a testament to deep change, human and wild.

—Terry Tempest Williams
author, *When Women Were Birds*

Daring, perceptive, and eloquent—Polson's writing is clear and forceful. Like all true pilgrimages, this one is challenging, and well worth taking.

—Scott Russell Sanders
author, *Earth Works* and *A Conservationist Manifesto*

Polson's extraordinary journey draws you into the depths of anguish and brings you back out realizing that while not all things fractured can be healed, the soul will gravitate toward beauty, art, and meaning if guided in the right direction.

—Alison Levine
mountaineer, polar explorer, and team captain
of the first American Women's Everest Expedition

North of Hope is an enthralling story of loss, courage, and redemption told by a gifted, original, and brave new voice, Shannon Huffman Polson.

—Robert Clark
award-winning author of ten books, including
Dark Water: Flood and Redemption in the City of Masterpieces
and *Mr. White's Confession*

As Shannon Polson poignantly recounts the loss of family members to a grizzly attack in the Arctic National Wildlife Refuge, framing her memoir around her own trek into the wilderness where they perished, she comes to believe that there is grace and wonder in the most unlikely places, that the landscape's wildness can teach you about letting go of control, and that Easter doesn't arrive until you've experienced Good Friday. Anyone who has endured the grief of losing someone or something they loved will identify with the advice Polson was given: "When tragedy comes into your life, the most beautiful thing you can do is keep moving forward."

—Cindy Crosby
former National Park Ranger and author of
By Willoway Brook: Exploring the Landscape of Prayer
(www.cindycrosby.com)

Shannon Polson brilliantly tells the story of venturing into the Alaskan wilderness to find the place where her parents were killed. Interwoven with that journey is the story of how she auditioned for and sang the Mozart Requiem. Only music could provide solace for her strange, almost unimaginable loss. This is no ordinary memoir. To read it is to be changed.

—Jeanne Walker
author, *New Tracks, Night Falling*

Shannon Huffman Polson has written a book about loss that is both unique to her personal experience and universal to the human experience. She writes with clarity, honesty, and poise. The end of her story has the surreal feel of fiction—a moment so unbelievable and fitting that it must have happened. Readers will find themselves caught up in that poetic end, and in the breadth of story that comes before it.

—Andrea Palpant Dilley
author, *Faith and Other Flat Tires:
Searching for God on the Rough Road of Doubt*

North of Hope, Shannon Polson's gripping account of the shattering, traumatic loss of her father, is a must read. In the end, Shannon is faced with a choice—does she choose the beauty and majesty of life or succumb to the pain and trauma of the loss of her beloved father? It is only after her father's death that she truly listens to, and embraces, his message—to believe in her own strength and to live a life of meaning and purpose. Shannon's book is a gift to everyone who reads this powerful, inspiring story.

—Janet Hanson
CEO and founder, 85 Broads

North of Hope is a remarkable story about the power of the wilderness both to harm and to heal, and to provide strength and sustenance to the human spirit, no matter what the challenges.

—Nicholas O'Connell
author, *The Storms of Denali*;
instructor, www.thewritersworkshop.net

NORTH OF HOPE

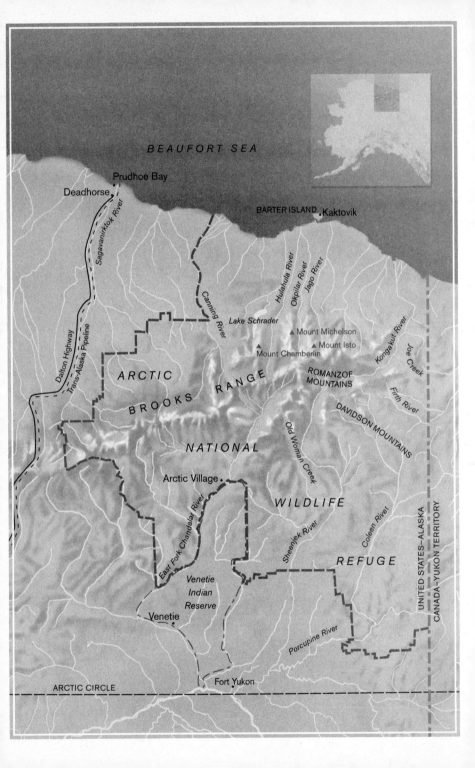

BEAUFORT SEA

Prudhoe Bay
Deadhorse

BARTER ISLAND •Kaktovik

Sagavanirktok River

Canning River

Hulahula River
Okpilar River
Jago River

Lake Schrader

▲ Mount Michelson
▲ Mount Isto
Mount Chamberlin ▲

Konga-kut River
Joe Creek

Dalton Highway
Trans-Alaska Pipeline

ARCTIC

BROOKS RANGE

ROMANZOF
MOUNTAINS

Firth River

DAVIDSON MOUNTAINS

NATIONAL

Old Woman Creek

Arctic Village •

WILDLIFE

East Fork Chandalar River

Sheenjek River

Coleen River

REFUGE

Venetie
Indian
Reserve

UNITED STATES–ALASKA
CANADA–YUKON TERRITORY

•Venetie

Porcupine River

ARCTIC CIRCLE

• Fort Yukon

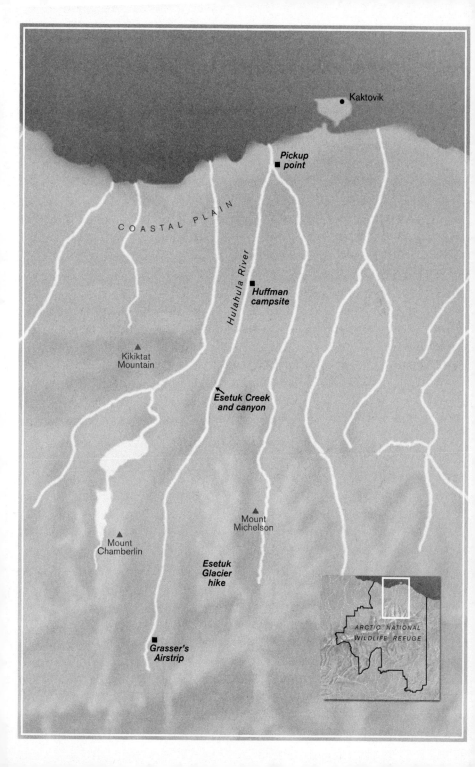

Kaktovik

Pickup point

COASTAL PLAIN

Hulahula River

Huffman campsite

Kikiktat Mountain

Esetuk Creek and canyon

Mount Michelson

Mount Chamberlin

Esetuk Glacier hike

Grasser's Airstrip

ARCTIC NATIONAL WILDLIFE REFUGE

SHANNON HUFFMAN POLSON

NORTH OF HOPE

A DAUGHTER'S ARCTIC JOURNEY

ZONDERVAN®

ZONDERVAN.com/
AUTHORTRACKER
follow your favorite authors

We want to hear from you. Please send your comments about this book to us in care of zreview@zondervan.com. Thank you.

ZONDERVAN

North of Hope
Copyright © 2013 by Shannon Huffman Polson

This title is also available as a Zondervan ebook.
Visit www.zondervan.com/ebooks.

This title is also available in a Zondervan audio edition.
Visit www.zondervan.fm.

Requests for information should be addressed to:

Zondervan, *Grand Rapids, Michigan* 49530

ISBN 978-0-310-32876-6

Published in association with David Jacobsen of Rivendell Literary (www.rivendellliterary.com).

The names and identifying characteristics of some people in this narrative have been changed. All events happened as told.

All references to indigenous beliefs came from primary and secondary source research. As these are subjects of great sensitivity, and more recent scholarship has expressed concern about the appropriateness of earlier research methodologies, my discussion is included in the narrative with the best of intentions and great respect to the peoples referenced and their beliefs.

Maps on pages 2 – 3 are from *Arctic National Wildlife Refuge: Seasons of Life and Land* © 2003 by Subhankar Banerjee. Used courtesy of Braided River.

Cover design: Studio Gearbox
Cover photography: Veer®
Map artist: Rose Michelle Taverniti
Interior design: Sarah Johnson

Printed in the United States of America

13 14 15 16 17 18 19 20 /DHV/ 21 20 19 18 17 16 15 14 13 12 11 10 9 8 7 6 5 4 3 2 1

FOR DAD AND KATHY

Who trusted God was love indeed
And love Creation's final law—
Tho' Nature, red in tooth and claw
With ravine, shriek'd against his creed—

...

O life as futile, then, as frail!
O for thy voice to soothe and bless!
What hope of answer, or redress?
Behind the veil, behind, the veil.

—Lord Alfred Tennyson, *In Memoriam*

My God my grief forgive my grief tamed in language
to a fear I can bear.
Make of my anguish
more than I can make. Lord, hear my prayer.

—Christian Wiman, "This Mind of Dying"

CONTENTS

ACKNOWLEDGMENTS

It is impossible to acknowledge the many people who have offered ideas and guidance over the many years it has taken to create *North of Hope*. I am overwhelmed by how generous so many were with their time and consideration in response to my frequent inquiries and requests for assistance on this long and uncertain journey.

Thank you to those willing to read the manuscript along the way: Emily Russin, Nan Mooney, and Sarah Delaney were readers of early sections, and Kyra Freestar edited an early version of the manuscript. Hugo House instructors Peter Mountford and Waverly Fitzgerald gave encouragement and excellent feedback on portions of the manuscript and proposal. Seattle Pro Musica director Karen P. Thomas lent me resources to research Mozart's Requiem in D Minor. Katey Schulz, Andy Schlickman, and Marcia Somers read later versions and helped me focus and hone my themes. A very special thanks to Hannah Moderow, who gave much time and substantial energy to look over the manuscript before I submitted it to make sure it was ready to fly.

Thank you to the excellent staff of the Anchorage Museum for research assistance; to the staff of the Elmer E. Rasmuson library at the University of Alaska Fairbanks for referrals to experts and research sources; to the staff at the Z. J. Loussac Library; and to the North Slope Borough Search and Rescue Division. Many thanks to Robert Thompson, resident and Arctic guide in Kaktovik, Alaska, for looking over a part of the manuscript for correctness; to Jim and Carol of Arctic Treks for their consultation on place name origins and geology; to Karen Jettmar of Equinox Expeditions for her review and consultation on several parts of the manuscript; and to Dr. Wesley Wallace from the University of Alaska Fairbanks Department of Geology and Geophysics for his expertise on the geology of the Romanzof Mountains and Arctic riparian ecosystems.

The Gwich'in Social and Cultural Institute provided invaluable assistance in research and the opportunity to talk to their elders. Thank you especially to Hannah Alexie and Catherine Mitchell.

I am indebted to my teachers and classmates in Seattle Pacific University's Master of Fine Arts program who have been fellow travelers and guides on this writing journey, and to my agent, David Jacobsen, who helped find a home for this manuscript.

I owe an eternal debt of gratitude to the vision of Carolyn Fonseca McCready and to the candid and careful attention of my editors, Dave Lambert and Brian Phipps, and to the rest of the team at Zondervan for their shepherding of this book to its final state.

And most of all I thank my husband, Peter, for his love and support to pursue my passion, and God, without whose grace none of this would have been possible.

....

CHAPTER 1

A SCARRED SKY

Hold my hand in this rupture of the planet
while the scar of a purple sky becomes a star.

– Pablo Neruda, *Canto General*

The plane fell from the clouds toward the dirt airstrip in the Inupiat village of Kaktovik, Alaska. I braced myself against the seat in front of me. Windows aged and opaque blurred the borders of ice and land, sea and sky. The airstrip rushed upward with menacing inevitability. Kaktovik perched on Barter Island, a barrier island shaped like a bison's skull just north of the Arctic Coastal Plain. Ice stretched from just offshore to the horizon. The Beech 1900 touched down with all the grace of a drunk, first one wheel and then the other staggering on the rough surface. Our bodies lurched forward and to the side. Gravel crunched beneath the wheels until the sound smoothed into a rhythmic bumping to the end of the runway.

As I walked off the plane down the rickety stairs, the Arctic wind cut through my fleece. I stood on the boundary between land and sea, water and ice. It was the end of the world. The ultima Thule.

As much as I pretended that courage motivated my trip, my arrival was a supplication born of a bewildering devastation I could not shake. I came on my knees, begging and desperate. Though I was reared in Alaska, this was my first trip to the Arctic.

But it was not the first day of this journey. This journey began a year ago, though I didn't then understand it, when the call came.

I was thirty-three years old, working in a new position in finance at a large company in Seattle. I didn't like finance, though I enjoyed working with my colleagues. I was smitten with a man named Peter, whom I had met three years earlier in business school in the Northeast. He was the first person I had ever thought I might marry. And then, on June 23, 2005, sitting on the couch of my Seattle apartment on a chilly summer evening, we decided things weren't working between us. I left early the next morning to drive to see my brother Sam and his wife in Portland, my dreams running down my face. That was Friday.

On Sunday, Sam, his wife, and I headed to the open-air market in Portland. A warm breeze wafted through the artists' stalls, and my sister-in-law and I strolled among the booths waiting for Sam to park and join us for lunch.

My phone rang, muffled, inside my purse. We reached the end of one row of artists' booths and turned the corner to walk down another. I fumbled around in my purse and silenced the ring, expecting to have plenty of time to talk on the three-hour drive home. From a distance, Sam ambled toward us, the same amble our dad had, all long strong legs. Walking among the artists' offerings, the three of us decided on lunch and sat at a picnic table to eat. The late morning sun settled around our shoulders as gently as a blanket. Around us drifted the laughter of children, the smell of cinnamon sugar and honey on elephant ears, and friendly flashes of color from wandering jesters with balloons.

As we returned to our cars, the pain of my breakup two days earlier suspended briefly in the cocoon of companionship, I said goodbye to Sam and his wife. I settled into my blue Jetta, turned the key, and smiled in the rearview mirror, holding my phone on my shoulder to listen to voicemail. I turned toward the highway, where I would leave my brother and his wife behind to head north.

Then the earth trembled.

The earth erupted.

"This is Officer Holschen from Kaktovik, Alaska, calling for Shannon Huffman. Please call me as soon as you get this message."

I didn't know the voice. I could barely comprehend the words. I pulled over. I called Sam and told him to pull over behind me, that I had just had a strange call. He jumped from his truck and strode to the passenger's side of my car. As he climbed into the passenger's seat — his frame, almost as tall as Dad's, filled it — I looked at my text messages and found a number with a 907 area code, indicating Alaska, and three additional numbers at the end: 911. My hand shook as I dialed. I couldn't remember my hand ever having been shaky before, but I couldn't stop the tremors.

"North Slope Borough," said the voice on the other end of the line.

There is a time in each of our lives when we are hurled into the terrible understanding that bedrock can crumble in the blink of an eye. And still, I felt a quiet and surprising steadiness, something wrapping itself around me to shield me from things to come. The shock protects you from the horror for a while, a brief respite from the cutting pain to come, a padding of grace. Even when you think you are feeling the pain, it has yet to begin.

"This is Shannon Huffman, returning Officer Holschen's call."

"Are you related to Richard and Katherine Huffman?" the voice asked.

"I'm Rich's daughter."

"I'm sorry to tell you this," said the voice, "but a bear came into their campsite last night ..."

Every part of what I thought I knew blazed like the brightest sun, extinguishing to blackness. The earth wobbled and spun out of orbit. Gravity no longer existed.

A flash of calculation appeared in the chaos, a shard of clarity thin and brittle as a sliver of glass: I had talked to Dad and Kathy the previous Sunday on Father's Day when they called on the satellite phone from a riverbank on the Hulahula River. They were fine, laughing, loving their trip. I would take care of them. I would need to make arrangements to get them to a hospital. I would need to talk to the doctors.

"... and they were both killed."

Exactly at that moment, Sam whispered, "Are they dead?" I nodded, all at once unbelieving, angry at the question, unable to breathe. In one prolonged instant, I vaguely felt the weight of Sam's head on my shoulder. I heard from him something like a sob. My breath caught in my throat. For a moment, time stood still. Cars driving by froze. People on the sidewalk halted midstep. Sounds hushed.

I'm not sure how I closed the conversation, the first of many, with Officer Holschen, but it had something to do with having bodies sent to Anchorage. I remember asking him not to release their names until we had had a chance to inform Kathy's family. I registered a muted note of surprise — anything I registered was muted, as though I were covered in a layer of foam — that I knew what questions to ask. The questions that were harder to ask, and impossible to answer, came later.

⋀

Now, only a year later, I arrived in the Arctic to float the Hulahula River, wishing I'd had a chance to say goodbye. Wishing I had spent more time with Dad and Kathy on rivers. Wishing for a sense of deeper connection to them. I had hoped Sam might come on this trip too, but he declined. He had immersed himself in distance cycling and had a 1200-kilometer ride scheduled while I was away on the river. Our brother Max was tied up at work in D.C. I had come feeling hollow, scooped out, empty. I had come because I knew I had to, though I couldn't articulate why.

I'd chosen my two traveling companions for their willingness to make the trip: my adopted brother, Ned, and his work colleague Sally. We stumbled down the shaky steps from the plane onto the frozen dirt runway in the island village of Kaktovik, the only settlement on the northern edge of Alaska between the Canadian border and Barrow. Our journey would start upriver along the Hulahula River on the mainland, just as Dad and Kathy's trip had, requiring a flight south on a yet smaller plane. But first we had to pick up our raft and other supplies.

The few other passengers from the flight to Kaktovik dispersed into the treeless landscape, and we stood alone under an overcast sky. Our loneliness was short-lived; within a few minutes of the plane's landing, a man named Ed, wearing a large mustache and a down coat, picked us up in a school bus that had seen better days. We each took our own seat; we were the only passengers. Ned sat rigidly even as the bus bumped over one of the town's handful of short dirt roads to the Waldo Arms Hotel, a group of derelict trailers and Quonset huts. Sally couldn't sit still in the bus seat. She had surprised me at our first meeting. I had heard only that she also kayaked, yet she was so plump as to appear almost round, with red smiling cheeks and dark blond hair pulled back in a ponytail.

"Wow! I can't believe we're finally here! Never thought I'd actually be in the Arctic!" Sally said. Her grin came easily, and I swallowed against how it chafed me. We were a motley crew, the three of us, I thought. To be embarking on a journey so personally significant with someone I didn't know seemed questionable at best.

Ned smiled something that looked more like a grimace, a second too late for spontaneity.

"Amazing," I said. Even to me my voice sounded flat.

I figured Sally must be smart; she worked with Ned in a market research firm back East. Ned and I had never been close. Growing up, we wore on each other like grinding gears. I assumed that adulthood had tempered his youthful angst, though we had not spent any significant time together in the years intervening. I had not wanted to come alone, and yet I hoped that neither Ned nor Sally would require me to engage with them. I wanted to have my own trip.

Outside of the dirty bus windows, the tiny houses of the village decayed into the landscape, brutalized by the harsh weather. They reminded me of old ice cubes left too long in the tray, withered in the subfreezing temperatures. No trees grew this far north, so the whole of the tiny village was visible. Old snowmobiles and broken dogsleds hunched in dirt yards, protected by mangy dogs straining at their chains outside the small homes. Other dogs slunk through the streets.

The bus bumped to a halt in front of Waldo Arms, which was barely distinguishable from the buildings around it. A moose skull and antlers and a Dall sheep skull, scoured white by wind and snow, sat outside the hotel doors. Clouds clustered about the mountains to the south when we arrived, threatening our afternoon departure plans, but there was still a lot to do. We would be renting a raft from Walt Audi, who ran Waldo Arms with his wife, Merilyn. Walt had been stationed in Kaktovik years ago as part of the Distant Early Warning (DEW) Line set up by Eisenhower in the late 1940s as the nation's primary air defense in case of a Russian invasion through Alaska. After that, he flew for years as one of Alaska's original bush pilots. A pile of bent propellers next to a shed by the airstrip attested to Walt's mythic indestructibility.

Ed worked with Walt and Merilyn. He took us through the drill of inflating the fourteen-foot blue rubber raft, checking the pressure and learning the pumps, practicing loading the raft with our enormous pile of coated nylon and rubber dry bags. As Ed gathered equipment, an Inupiat woman came to stand in the doorway and told stories of going far out onto the ice to hunt walrus. Ed pulled out a scale, and we weighed the gear, including the raft:

440 pounds. The pilot needed to know this so he could decide how many trips to make to ferry us and our gear to our put-in point. We bought white fuel for our camp stoves from Ed, disassembled the raft, and loaded the truck with our gear to go back to the airfield.

Our preparation was complete, but clouds still hung heavily over the mountains. The last weather call grounded us until the next day. Even if one could find shelter from the elements in this tiny village teetering on the edge of the world, there was never any question that nature ruled. We were forced to slow down, to take nature on her own terms. The start of our trip on the Hulahula would have to wait. We were in Kaktovik for the night.

Waldo Arms had a monopoly on lodging, and a room ran a couple of hundred dollars a night, well beyond our trip budget. We opted for the bunkhouse at forty dollars a night. Bunkhouse was a euphemistic term: behind the Quonset hut of the hotel was an uninsulated and unlit plywood shed with filthy mattresses piled on top of each other on rudimentary bunks. A narrow gangplank connected the bunkhouse to the rest of the Waldo Arms trailers. Ragged Visqueen covering the broken glass of a window let in some light.

"Well, it's probably too cold for bugs," I said to no one in particular.

"Hope so," said Sally, maintaining what I thought was remarkable composure for an East Coast city girl in a remote Alaskan village. She began arranging her gear.

Dropping my backpack and sleeping bag on one of the bare mattresses, I walked up the gangplank and headed into the common area of Waldo Arms. Inside, I sank into an ancient gold floral velvet couch and took in the room around me. The couch sat on a rust-colored carpet well scuffed by boots over the years. A large piece of scrimshawed baleen hung on the wall above a notice of the musk ox hunt, warnings about polar bears roaming the village, maps of Alaska, and assorted articles and calendars about Alaska and the Arctic from past decades. Static and the occasional voice scratched an uneven staccato over the radio in the office at the far end of the room. A small window into the kitchen with a laminated menu beside it offered expensive greasy food, and a couple of picnic tables covered in red-and-white-checkered vinyl tablecloths sat in the dining area. In the kitchen, the gentle cacophony of clanging pans was strangely soothing in its familiarity. As my body relaxed into the couch, all of the details that had insulated me for so long — the decision to come, organizing the trip, the preparation before departure which had filled the time and the crevices of my mind — evaporated like the Arctic coastal fog in the summer midnight sun. Now my mind focused with a clarity that, while not welcome, was inevitable.

On June 14, 2005, a little over a year ago, I had received the last email I would ever see from Dad:

> Hi all. I know you don't need all this but here it is: we leave on the 15th on Frontier Flying service to Barter Island. If the weather is good, we fly the same day to Grasser's on the Hulahula River. We have a good orange tent, two inflatables (red and yellow), extra paddles, food for 17 days, first aid stuff, dry suits, helmets, pfds, sat phone, gps and vhf radio. We plan to take two weeks goofing off and paddling down river for a pickup at the coast on the 29th and fly back to Fairbanks that night. Then to cabin for a couple of days. We fly from the village of Kaktovik on Barter Island with Alaska Flyers. Their phone is 907-640-6324 — owner is Walt and pilot is Tom. The satellite phone is with Iridium through Surveyor's exchange at 561-6501. You guys be safe and well. I love you and I am very proud of each of you! Kathy sends her best! love, Dad

I hadn't noticed the detail they'd given. Details we would need to look for them, to identify a campsite. Last year they had been in this same place, excited, preparing, checking equipment. Perhaps they had sat on the same couch.

The possibilities and wonderings pressed in, soft and firm like chloroform; I needed to move. Ned and Sally stayed behind to read, but I needed the feel of ground beneath my boots. I zipped up my coat and headed through the set of double doors. Outside, a barbed wind scratched at my face and penetrated my fleece. I welcomed the distraction. I headed toward the police station.

Though most of the scattered buildings of the village cowered from the ferocity of Arctic weather, the government buildings, funded by oil companies, stood solidly. At the police station, I walked into the welcome of a well-lit room, entering the concrete edge of the story I had been sketching for a year. Officer Holschen, the policeman who had first called me, had fielded my calls many times in the intervening months, rehashing details and events.

"Where exactly were they on the beach?"

"How do you know how long they had been dead?"

"Have you seen bears act this way with other people?"

"Can you tell exactly what killed them?"

"Where was the emergency locater beacon? Had they tried to use it?"

A thousand other questions had burped rudely into my mind, never at opportune moments. Each time, I called Officer Holschen, and each time, he answered patiently, talked through my questions, never impatient, never annoyed. His life and line of work had taught him to understand the survivor's need to pick up each rock and turn it over again and again and again. He understood the human delusion that believes that if we can answer questions, fill in the story, somehow we might turn back the clock.

Officer Holschen was strangely real. The mental character sketch I had engaged with in the story of Dad's and Kathy's deaths deepened suddenly into a real person. He greeted me with a big hug. His first name was Richard, the same as Dad's. I had expected him to be a native man, because Kaktovik is a native village. Instead, he was Caucasian, about my height with light brown hair and an easy smile, his uniform neatly pressed and tucked. Looking at him, a real man instead of only a voice with a name, I was astonished to think of myself as dimensional too, another character walking through the same story from a different angle. I had become accustomed to considering myself an empty shell, chasing ghosts and shadows.

"I came to raft the Hulahula," I said, feeling my face flush. Speaking the words underscored the audacity of undertaking a trip of such immensity. I was suddenly embarrassed, as though I'd been caught playing dress-up as a child. My words to Officer Holschen that day made me fully aware, for the first time, of the journey ahead. So much about the past year was so unreal, so intangible, that I had ceased to understand context. "Just thought I'd come by and say hello, and thank you in person for all the help you were to me over the past year."

We confirmed my coordinates with his from the police report. "Has anyone had any more ideas on the bear last year?" I asked.

Officer Holschen shook his head. "But you know, I don't know that bears are so different from people. There are people out there who are crazy, and who's to say there aren't animals with the same problem? If I were to give it my best guess, I would say that this was just a rogue bear."

"We brought along the 45-70 and a shotgun with slugs," I said. "What do you recommend if a bear approaches?"

"They rarely take notice of you. But if they do approach aggressively, ninety-nine percent of the time they'll run away if you fire at the ground so it sprays up in front of them."

"What if they don't?" I asked.

"If they keep coming after the first shot, aim for anything brown," he said. "But I've never seen that happen."

We said our goodbyes. "It's great to meet you," he said with a big smile. "Have a wonderful trip!"

Outside, I realized that I had reached the end of the dirt road. I headed back toward the beach, where the Inupiat villagers were holding their June whaling festival, Nalukataq, a thanksgiving celebration following their spring whaling season.

Along a makeshift wall of Visqueen and plywood, villagers hunkered down out of the frigid Arctic wind blowing off of the polar ice. Weathered brown hands offered passersby bits of pinkish-white blubber attached to thick black whale skin cut into pieces one or two inches long, a delicacy called *muktuk*.

A couple staying at Waldo Arms was roaming the party as well. "It's an acquired taste," they said with a smile as I looked a moment too long at the cold gelatinous mass, "but it's not bad with plenty of ketchup!"

A smiling Inupiat woman in a colorful and ornately stitched parka held out a piece of muktuk on a white paper plate. There was kindness in her deep-set eyes, the creases in her face holding years of weather and wisdom. I took the paper plate with the gift of whale and added a liberal dose of ketchup, popping a piece in my mouth before letting myself think about it. The muktuk was disconcertingly rubbery. I suppressed a gag and chewed until it was gone, not quite able to disguise my distaste.

Officer Holschen and a couple of his children walked by with plates of muktuk, which they clearly were enjoying. "They say it's a kind of fat that keeps you warm if you eat enough of it," he said, smiling. "They love this stuff here. We've really grown to like it, especially the kids!" I smiled back at the happy family.

I was an intruder here. These people living in a remote village with traditions so vastly different from any I had known made up the only culture that could understand the land I presumed to visit with my unarticulated plea for peace. They lived the connections among people and animals, earth and sea. The Inupiat were the only ones equipped to understand any answers. I was a stranger, an outsider. I had accepted their gift of hospitality, participated in village tradition, and had nothing to offer in return. I didn't know then to accept it as grace.

Before embarking on this journey, I had considered my impending intrusion into the wilderness. But only after visiting the village celebration was I aware of my double trespass. I hoped that a people so close to the land possessed a deeper understanding than I about animals, about animals killing loved ones, about how to navigate this primal and unforgiving world. I hoped I might learn at least some of that understanding from them. Perhaps it could mitigate the pain. Perhaps it would help me honor even more those I had lost.

Walking back to Waldo Arms, I realized I had a piece of whale skin stuck in my teeth and worked on getting it out. It was persistent. It took my mind off the wind.

Back inside, I curled into an overstuffed blue plaid chair and pulled out the five map sheets Dad and Kathy had used to float the river. The paper was soft as worn felt. The maps led from Grasser's Airstrip to the coast. Alaska — North Slope Borough, Mt. Michelson Quadrangle, 1:63,360 series, topographic. United States Department of the Interior Geological Survey. Maps indicate, among many things, a declination angle showing the variance from true north to magnetic north; earth's magnetic fields skew a compass reading from true north as indicated on maps. Without taking this variance into account, a person could end up far from her destination. Our best understanding of direction is far removed from earth's reality. On maps I had used before, the declination angle might be five or even seven degrees. This far north, the maps indicated an astonishing mean declination of thirty-five degrees from true north. Reconciling the different realities, the different "norths," would require huge adjustments.

My fingers traced a tear in one of the maps. A rip from regular use, or from the bear rampaging through the campsite? I had asked that the police destroy anything from the campsite that was mauled by the bear, terrified of opening a box containing blood-soaked shreds of nylon. But in the box of what remained from the campsite sent by the police, several things arrived intact. I used the map case Dad and Kathy had used to hold maps, their book of Alaska's wildflowers, and a waterproof REI journal. Now I flipped through Dad and Kathy's journal, as I had so many times before. They had alternated entries, in Kathy's smooth hand and Dad's almost unintelligible scrawl. Since they measured their progress by how far north they had traveled on the river, the latitude and date began each entry, the longitude determined by the course of the river. I marked each of their camps along the river and numbered the maps in order of use. I was glad for my extensive experience in map reading during years of flying helicopters in the army. This was the first opportunity I had had to mark a route on a map since my last flight, six years earlier.

As I sat with the contents of the map case, the present intruded uncomfortably on the past. What was I doing here? How did I think I was in any way qualified for this trip? I had never been to the Arctic. And the physical risks were the least of my concerns. I'd become good at taking those risks over the years. But as much as I had sought adventure, I had avoided emotional connection, a protective mechanism I had perfected rapidly after my mom left the family when I was twelve. Perpetual motion excused avoiding emotional engagement. This expedition, though, was taking me to one of the most remote areas of the world, and also to the darkest recesses of my pain. I didn't have nearly enough experience in that landscape. My resolve flickered like a flame in a gusty wind. I willed the wick to hold on to that tiny flame. It was all I had.

CHAPTER 2

RESTLESS WATERS

The landscape and the language are the same.
And we ourselves are landscape and are land.
–Conrad Aiken, "A Letter from Li Po"

Waldo Arms housed a varied crowd. We crossed paths at the picnic tables in the dining area. A researcher, a couple of photographers, someone who recorded bird sounds. Some were interested in the native culture, and others did not try to hide their disapproval of native practices. All expressed strong opinions on the wilderness, Alaskan wilderness guides, and animal biology. Several suggested far from subtle agendas. Though I was not overt about the reason for our trip, the extended conversations we had during the weather delay, characterized by rare and probing honesty made possible only in times and places marked by remoteness, rapidly unveiled everyone's circumstances, including my own.

Each meal came with a serving of unsolicited opinion about the bear last year. "He must have been a garbage bear," one naturalist confided with wrinkled brow. "Prudhoe Bay gets bears accustomed to people with all of their trash." A couple of birders peered at me intently. "It's the native fish camps," they said, as though confiding a deep secret. "They leave trash all over the tundra, and the bears are used to people having food." Each suggestion validated someone's agenda; none were verifiable. Certainly none of them changed the outcome.

Our pilot, Tom, who had flown Dad and Kathy into Grasser's Airstrip, came into the dining room after dinner. His graying hair and beard framed the weathered eyes of someone who has peered long into Alaska's unknown.

"Anyone up for a polar bear swim?" he asked with a chuckle. "A German photographer did it last year!"

"Sounds cold," I said.

"You sure you don't want to go?"

Not only was I reluctant to submerse myself in an ice bath with polar bears, I wasn't particularly interested in goofing off. This was not how I wanted to begin a trip fraught with so much meaning, even meaning I couldn't quite define.

"Come on—the photographer did it! I recorded it! Watch this!"

Merilyn came into the room and leaned against the wall with a smile. "I think Tom was a little sweet on her," she said.

Tom inserted a videotape into an ancient VCR, and the unlikely image of a pretty, laughing woman rushing into the icy ocean appeared on the old TV. She sprinted out as soon as she was in, and someone wrapped her in a towel. Laughter came from behind the camera, and the picture gave way to static.

"Brave," I said, feeling a little inadequate.

"You sure you don't want to swim?" The footage grayed out.

"I think I'm okay. I need to stay healthy for the river!" I smiled weakly, hoping my excuse would hold.

The fuzzy picture on the TV took form again with the faraway sound of rotor blades. We glanced back at the TV.

"Oh," Tom said, and then he stiffened suddenly. His reaction, even fleeting, ricocheted throughout the room like a warning shot. We were not supposed to see what followed.

The tape showed a helicopter landing in fog so thick it seemed to muffle the sound of the rotor blades as they swung slowly to a stop, making a noise like a low bass chord on a piano. On the screen, the door of the helicopter opened and the pilot stepped out.

Though details were obscured by the low light and fog, his every physical aspect manifested solemnity.

"This is last year, the day they found your folks," Tom said slowly. His confirmation of the obvious entered me like a cutting and consuming cold. I was exposed again to the elements, to the formidable forces threatening to subsume me. I was vaguely aware of a terror of the dark jokes that people make during uncomfortable circumstances — or an unseemly filming of all aspects of an event, no matter how gruesome or disturbing. But the pilot's voice was barely audible on the videotape, deeply somber. And respectful.

The tape jumped to the next morning: an aerial view of the coastal plain, early morning sunshine deepening the rich greens of the tundra. I sucked my cheeks against my teeth. The tape showed a final view of the parked helicopter, shining white in the low-angle light, and then reverted to static. I relaxed. The few recorded scenes displayed a quiet respect for the circumstances and for Dad and Kathy. This community had a deep and elemental experience of tragedy. Natives and non-natives alike, Alaskans have a respect for the wilderness and for their own who venture into it, responding with an appropriate sense of gravity, and yet acceptance, when their adventurers do not return.

"Well, I think that's about it," Tom said.

"Do you think we could get a copy of that?" I asked.

"Sure thing," Tom said.

As part of Nalukataq, the villagers had planned a dance for the evening. I headed again into the cold toward the community center, taking a seat with the few other non-natives in metal folding chairs against the far wall. Smiling children in tiny *mukluks*—embroidered boots made of skins—pranced across the floor, dancing with the happy abandon available only to small children, immersed in the joy of the moment and innocent of life's losses. In the first row of chairs across the room, several men struck *qilaut*, large flat drums, with sticks, the stretched skin surfaces responding with an intense resonance to the varied rhythms and force. Heavy vowel sounds emanated from deep in the men's throats. People flowed in and out of the center of the room with exaggerated steps, reaching for the sky, gesturing to the ground. The music, the singing, the dancing seemed to invoke centuries of tradition and storytelling, prayer and incantation.

I sat awash in the energy of the room. The throaty vowels of the singers rode on the drumbeats, pulsing in the air. Somehow it seemed that these rhythms might connect dots in the picture I was trying to understand, that they might unlock a door into part of the mystery. It is said that Native American drums are the heartbeat of the world. I had forgotten my own heartbeat, but suddenly there was a fluttering at my throat.

In the Inuit (the circumpolar peoples of which the Inupiat are a part) dualistic metaphysical understanding, each person has a breath soul and a free soul. The breath soul gives life to a person, and after death becomes a name soul to protect later generations. The free soul might be located in the body or follow like a shadow. The individual breath soul is part of the cosmic breath soul, or *Sila*, also thought of as a creative life force.[1] Words, spoken and especially sung, are expressions of this breath soul. From breath to song, the soul emerges. The cosmos speaks. If I could learn to hear it.

Every fall, the Inuit must find new songs as they prepare for feasts honoring the whale. Men go into the festival house, where no lamps can be lit. They sit in darkness and stillness and something called *qarrtsiluni*, meaning that one waits for something to happen. All men are involved, from the youngest able to speak to the oldest. They sit in this darkness and this stillness thinking only of beautiful things. As they do this, songs rise like bubbles in the sea seeking the surface, where they explode into air.[2]

Everything is connected. In trying to understand an event so seemingly inexplicable and yet so much of the wilderness itself, as were Dad and Kathy's deaths, I had to believe this, even if I did not feel it. I had to believe in some sort of an order so that chaos would not overwhelm me. But I didn't understand it. Not at all.

The party showed no signs of slowing, so at nine o'clock I quietly headed back to the bunkhouse to rest for the next day, walking on the frozen dirt roads under skies dimmed to an early twilight. I maneuvered down the gangplank into the bunkhouse, where Ned and Sally were already asleep, and wiggled into my sleeping bag atop the dingy mattress, closing my eyes against the filtered light.

Sleep was not to last long. An hour later, I blinked awake to banging on the makeshift door.

"There's a polar bear at the bone pile!" a voice I quickly identified as belonging to our pilot, Tom, yelled. "We're leaving in three minutes to take a look!"

"You guys going to go?" I asked quietly, unzipping my sleeping bag.

"Nope," mumbled Sally, not moving.

"Yeah, of course!" said Ned.

Even in the middle of the night, a dawn-like light filtered through the cracks in the walls and broken windows, allowing just enough vision to quickly throw on polypropylene and hiking boots, which I did in about forty-five seconds. Despite the light, the air was frigid, as though the brightness lost from the day had stolen along with it all semblance of warmth, and the light breeze off the polar ice clawed at our bare faces. Along with six other intrepid tourists, Ned and I piled into an old Suburban. Tom sped down the gravel road, around the gravel airstrip, and past the aircraft hangars, bumping toward the pile of whale bones on the far edge of the village.

Ice extended to the horizon from just offshore, and but for the thin strip of water that separated the island from the ice, glistening black in the low light, the ice might have been a continuation of the land. Here were two worlds apart, yet one. The bone pile, a record of successful autumn whaling expeditions, stood terrible against the white background. Countless bones, many larger than the Suburban, were silhouetted eerily in the soft light. And then we saw the bear. At first it was only a movement behind the bone pile, a shift in the landscape. And then his form emerged. His head was sleek as a seal, his Brobdingnagian body shaped smooth as a river-worn rock, all slopes and soft edges. He wore his sovereignty easily. Paws the size of dinner platters meant for swimming Arctic seas rummaged through hunks of whale fat among the bones, the same whale fat we had eaten as muktuk earlier that day. The bear looked toward the Suburban only briefly, more interested in finding his meal. We kept a reverent distance, each of us prickling with awareness and cold. Bodies hung out of every car window; freezing fingers pressed camera shutters. The bear lumbered toward us, swaying gently, then moved away again. He bore with surety the incongruity of ultimate power and a dancer's lissome grace. I envied him his perfect design, his complete confidence in his body, his surroundings, his world. He was as elegant, as fluid, as water as he scavenged for sustenance among the remains of the dead.

Inuits believe that the bear is special. Every animal species has a collective breath soul, except for the bear, the whale, and the dog, which have individual breath souls. While most ceremonies related to animals are devoted to the entire species, those that celebrate the bear are devoted to the soul of the individual bear. The polar bear spirit Torngarsuk can be, as with grizzlies, part of a ritual for shamanic initiation involving the initiate's reduction to a skeleton and then reconstitution as a shaman. Death, and resurrection into sacred life. Inuit in other parts of the world have considered the bear spirit the ruler of the afterlife, and other northern cultures have considered it a guide for souls.

Reduction. Reconstitution. How does one in the midst of reduction maintain faith in reconstitution? Quarrtsiluni. Waiting.

Three times the bear moved toward the front of the bone pile and in our direction. Soon he lost interest in the remains and, thankfully, in us. He slipped smoothly into the dark water, gliding up onto a piece of ice, back into the water, and up onto another ice floe. And then, in the ethereal glow of Arctic midnight, he disappeared.

Our proximity to this creature awakened something in me ancient and deep and wild. It did not rouse in me any acute feelings of fear; instead it validated my reason for coming to this edge of the world, this margin of place and time. It served as both warning and welcome. I had arrived in the wilderness.

⋀

Morning came with clear skies for travel. Because of the combined weight of our gear and bodies, the Cessna made two trips. The first load with Sally, Ned, and our raft took off for Grasser's Airstrip.

Sitting alone in the tattered surrounds of Waldo Arms, I waited for the crackling voice from the radio to announce that the Cessna had returned for me — alone, where only a year ago Dad had sat in khaki river pants and black fleece coat, next to Kathy in her matching khaki pants and light-blue fleece, the same fleece I wore on this trip, though it was a size too big. I held their yellow journal in my hands, the same one I'd read through so many times in the past year. I opened it:

June 2005

Hulahula River
Pilot # 907.640.6513 Walt
VHF Channel 10 Freq 122.9
St Troopers 1.800.478.9112
Tundra Strip Coor: N 69 58.906 W 144 01 306
Tom's Sat phone 8816 3157 1763
6-15-05 4:50 AM
Bags: Ak Air Flight

K's net bag
R's net bag
2 blue float bags
1 orange float bag
1 ski bag
1 red kayak
1 yellow kayak
1 yellow cargo bag
1 red cargo bag
Gun case
Ammo? Med Bag?

June 15, 2005 At Grassers +2400 Ev 69 05 N — looks like 23–24 miles in mountains then all coastal plains to coast … Flew down the Hulahula drainage. All around Barter and the delta is wet!!! Reshuffle then onto 206 and Tom Johnson for Audi. Really nice plane — great pilot. Beautiful day — lots of wind. A great treat to be here with Kathy. Rich (P.S. saw musk ox, big wolf and a bunch of sheep and lambs).

I was beginning the same trip they had started a year before. But while the geography and mode of travel were identical, nothing else about this trip was similar. This was not simply a trip into the wilderness, though that would be challenge and adventure enough. This was a journey over the jagged edge of loss. Despite the maps I had carefully marked and folded and stored in plastic cases, it was a trip into uncharted territory. The emptiness of the Quonset hut enveloped me, and I could not escape the awareness of much bigger voids.

The radio crackled again.

Merilyn came out of the office. "Okay, you're up!" she said. "He'll be here in a minute."

"Thanks!"

She paused. "I still feel them here, you know."

"You do?"

"Sure. My mother stayed around for several years after she died. I think sometimes they'll do that until they're ready to go to the next place."

"That makes sense," I said, willing to believe it. Nothing else made sense to me anymore, and I wanted to feel Dad and Kathy too.

I put their journal into the waterproof map case with my empty journal, the maps, and the book on Alaskan wildflowers, stood up and collected my bags, and walked out into the wind.

Requiem

Kyrie

Lord, suffer me to sing
these wounds by which I am made
and marred

—Christian Wiman, "Lord Is Not a Word"

I do not know if song came before prayer, or prayer before song, but I do know that together they are magnified and soar as they cannot do alone. Hebrew and Greek have no separate word for music, nor does the language of the Inupiat; the boundary between singing and speech wavers like a mirage.[3] I come to song to help me pray, and I come to prayer to help me sing. Sitting in a rehearsal room in a hard metal folding chair every Monday in Seattle after Dad and Kathy's funeral, I start to sing. I start to pray. I do not know yet that music will lead me to a river.

The chorale director stands in front of plate glass windows overlooking Lake Union and the headlights of I-5, slicing through the dark night. Rehearsal is a torrent of voices, each part channeling and eddying, rising to a frenzied pitch. The words are not hard. There are only three: "Kyrie eleison.

Christe eleison." Lord, have mercy. Christ, have mercy. The music carries the words. The words carry the music.

My score of Mozart's Requiem in D Minor is well used. I wonder if the singers who wore the pages to this petal softness held it with as much hope as I do, opened it with such expectation laced with trepidation and desire. It is a holy book, this score, this pathway to prayer. I sit and I sing and I feel lucky to be here, doing the only new thing I've been able to take on since I came back from Alaska after the funeral and selling my childhood home; it's the thing I needed to do, though I could not have said that myself.

It had happened in a slow, quiet way, my getting to that hard metal folding chair. In the midst of grief's restlessness and languor, I'd opened a flyer that came in the mail from the Seattle Symphony, advertising a performance of the Mozart Requiem conducted by Itzhak Perlman five months hence. I pulled up the Symphony Chorale page online and looked at audition schedules. They were two weeks away. I signed up.

The word *requiem* comes from the Latin, meaning "to rest," and the Requiem Mass is a service for the dead in the Christian tradition. It is a structure of prayers that has varied over the ages, depending on the history of the church and the intention of the composer, and it has been set to music many times, perhaps most famously by Mozart.

A gentle introduction and the Kyrie begin the Requiem Mass: "Lord have mercy upon us." From there it moves into the terror of the Dies Irae, or Day of Wrath. This part of the Requiem departs from the standard Mass sequence and was first added in the fourteenth century because of its vivid imagery, a nod to the inability of our daily prayers to fully express our grief. The Domine Jesu asks God to bless those we have lost. The Sanctus and Benedictus praise God, and the Agnus Dei begs God's mercy. The Lux Aeterna pleads for everlasting light to shine on the dead.

Singing the Requiem for Dad and Kathy could be the ritual I

thought I was missing. *If* I could get into the Symphony Chorale. The thing was, I had a hard time concentrating on much. My mind floated listlessly, as though in a mountain fog. How could I start something new when I could barely put one foot in front of the other?

Perhaps it had not been slow and quiet after all. Perhaps it happened fiercely, a propulsion of pain. Who's to say how these things happen? But the flyer I received, and the audition that followed, lined up as though orchestrated from another place, by a bigger hand, in the careful way that even when you do not feel him, God moves gently in your life.

The conductor rehearses the men through a section. I sit and listen. The folding chairs around me are full of people, most of whom I don't know, some of whom might consider the words they are singing, some of whose only interest in the words is their proper pronunciation, the intonation of vowels. Some are Christian, some Jewish, some atheist, and, I imagine, others are of different beliefs yet. Some are here for the music, and some are here for prayer. I am here for both. I need the music to pierce me, the prayer to bleed me. I am here because I don't know what to say, how to ask, how to address this God I've known for so long when parts of me are dead. I know only that I need to pray. And I need the music to do it for me. I need the music to pull me into the time called *kairos*, unbound by clocks and calendars, to give me courage to stay with the pain and help me pray this ancient prayer.

Kyrie eleison. Christe eleison.

CHAPTER 3

THE VALLEY
OF THE SHADOW

Yea, though I walk through the valley of the shadow of death, I will fear
no evil.

—Psalm 23:4

The Cessna's wheels broke from the gravel strip, leaping into
the arms of a blue sky. We swung in a sweeping circle over
Kaktovik. The change in perspective lent elegance to the meager
cluster of dwellings surrounded by dark water and white ice, the
Arctic Coastal Plain reaching out to the south, and beyond it,
the mountains beckoning. Rising at last from the ground should
have been a relief, an escape, but I felt nothing. Every time wheels
left the ground in the years I flew helicopters, or rode in a small
plane, I'd felt a surge of possibility; this time my eyes glazed over
and my chest felt as frozen as the permafrost below, that layer of
frozen soil that never thaws, that prevents roots from going deep,
so that the only vegetation is close to the surface.

From our take-off point, we flew west to the delta of the Hulahula River, then turned and followed it south, overflying the route
my two companions and I would be floating. I looked down at the
gentle weave of watery channels that had already submerged me,
already rolled me across their boulders.

Tom scanned the landscape with his keen eyes, the eyes of a

pilot who has looked into years of sky and can see a prophecy in a wisp of cloud. He made light conversation. He was looking for weather; I was trying to see the future, while traveling to the past. I bantered back more stodgily, feeling an acidic tightening in my stomach. The sky revealed nothing to me.

My family, especially on Dad's side, had not received the news of this trip happily. None of our family living in Kansas and Arizona understood the Alaskan — or the outdoors — mentality. As far as they were concerned, any trip away from the comforts of home was a dance on the knife-edge of fate. "Now honey, you'd better be safe," my aunt said, not so much a plea as a demand. "You do everything you need to do to be sure you come back." I had every intention of coming back. But of course, flying in a year ago, so had Dad and Kathy.

I have always been told I take after my dad, and I have been proud of it. But that similarity also meant we clashed as I was growing up. As with most first children, especially first children who are girls, I was given more rules to follow than my brothers, who came after me. One evening I came home an hour after curfew on what had been a particularly difficult day at school. Though I was staying at my mom's house — my parents had divorced a few years before — Dad sat waiting for me on the couch. I was in high school long before cell phones, and there had been no way to find me. After hearing in detail how he had spent his last hour — driving roads searching for me, calling the police, checking hospitals — I went to bed tired and chastened, and saw him a short four hours later when I was awakened to go to work with him. I nodded off over filing cabinets and struggled to stay awake changing out the supplements of law journals. The intention of the punishment was instructive — to understand the impact of my actions on others.

Dad didn't reveal his concern after my sophomore year of college, when I announced that I would climb Denali, the tallest mountain in North America and an adventure that turned out to be a three-week expedition on her icy flanks, or when I told him that I would get my commission in the army along with my English degree from Duke and fly attack helicopters. He sometimes wrote me on yellow legal paper in a hand only his secretary could read reliably — and his family, most of the time. In those letters he offered any number of exhortations: to be honest, to act ethically, to dress classically, to keep up with an exercise routine.

When I was climbing Denali, Dad asked our pilot, Lowell Thomas, whom we knew from church, to fly around the mountain and report on our team's status. Or perhaps Lowell had volunteered. Either way, he checked on us during our three weeks on the glacier and called in the all-okay to Dad.

At home in Alaska for Christmas after I returned from an army deployment to Bosnia, Lowell greeted me as he always did after the midnight service and said, "You know, your father was really worried about you when you were over there."

The gravity in Lowell's voice, the intentness of his eyes, surprised me. Dad never mentioned being worried when I called on the sat phone from the tactical operations center at Tuzla West. Hearing that Dad had worried meant the world to me.

My last year in the army, Dad came to visit me in the border town of El Paso, Texas, where I was stationed developing doctrine for Theater Missile Defense Joint Forces Targeting. Dad had been stationed in El Paso briefly himself and remembered it with no affection, but I loved the desert mountains and training for triathlons with a group of civilian friends. Dad and I went for hikes in the mountain valleys and visited Hueco Tanks to see the ancient petroglyphs. We tried Mexican restaurants around town.

One evening, we drove a long windy road up one side of the Franklin Mountains while the heat of the day settled onto the desert horizon red like blood and a towering bank of clouds galloped over the ridgeline like a herd of wild horses. "I've always hoped you kids would go to graduate school," he said, his eyes on the road ahead of us, and I recognized in his voice his small-town Kansas insecurities. Even as a successful attorney thousands of miles and tens of years away, he still spoke in the voice of post-Depression Midwest fear, in the voice of hope for his children, in the voice of judgment on himself as a parent. If there is one legacy parents are destined to pass on to their children, no matter their intentions, it is their insecurities.

Dad's message was one I had already internalized. A month later I received my acceptance letter to the Tuck School at Dartmouth, where I'd sent my application from Kuwait. My application packet had arrived in Hanover the last day of the last round of admissions. I called Dad the moment I got back to my apartment. He left a meeting to take my call, as he had when I'd called after my first jump at Airborne School ten years before. "Dad, I got in!" I remember saying.

He chuckled — I remember that — and said, "Well, that's no surprise. Congratulations, kiddo. What do you think?"

What did I think? It was a way to get back into the world. It validated me in a way the army no longer did. "I don't know — I'm excited!"

"Well, just make sure that you take time to think about this. Don't make a decision based on ego," Dad said. I was surprised at his caution, and though I knew I should be grateful for it, I didn't restrain my enthusiasm.

I talked to a friend who had made the transition from the army to business school. "This is the last decision I want to make for my dad," I said. "Then I need to figure out what I want to do." I was wrong; it took years to rid myself of the need to please my dad, a need knit into every part of my neural network.

I accepted Tuck's offer of admission and went to business school. That fall I became ill. It was early in the year, and I didn't know anyone well. I lived off campus, so without classmates nearby, I drove myself to the emergency room. Apparently the hospital IT systems weren't functioning, because Dad called the hospital from Alaska, only to be told that I wasn't registered. Then he called the police, worried that I may have driven into the ditch on icy roads, and asked them to go by my apartment to make sure I wasn't still there. One of the thoughts I could never shake the year after he died was that I no longer had anyone to check on me, no one making sure I was okay. Who would ever know what might happen to me, and who would care?

I lived for his attention. More than anything, I wanted my dad to be proud of me. That's the thing about a strong father: I learned strength from him, but for much of my earlier life I had a hard time discerning the difference between pleasing him and living for myself. He would have been disappointed about that.

The past few years had not been easy between Dad and Kathy and me. Dad had visited me by himself every year previously, sleeping on the pullout couch in my living room, but after that visit to El Paso, he started bringing Kathy with him and staying in a hotel. Instead of starting our day with an early breakfast, as we had with just the two of us, they sauntered up after she had finished a long yoga practice. When I told him my business school graduation date, he responded carefully: "I'll have to see what our schedule looks like. Kathy's niece is graduating college."

I told him the date of my first Ironman triathlon, which coincided in time and place with a river trip he and Kathy were planning to take in Idaho. "We'll see how the schedule works out," he said. I was hurt and responded with childish frustration, not calling him until he called me, even weeks later.

Visiting home that Christmas, a large photo of a friend's child sat framed on the kitchen counter. There were no photos of us kids.

"I come home once a year, and there's a picture of some random person on the counter?" I said, knowing it was probably Kathy who had set it there, demonstrating that her priorities mattered too. I wasn't interested in her priorities. "Don't you think your own kids deserve that kind of attention?" I pushed and pushed.

I don't remember all of that conversation, but I do remember it ending in the living room. "Every day of my life, I remember the days each of you were born!" Dad said, exasperated. "I remember you growing up. I remember everything!"

That's all I had wanted to hear. A victory, bought at the cost of civility and trust, penalties that would be exacted on other visits. I wondered what had gone wrong.

I bought a book on reconnecting with fathers. I considered Kathy warily. They came to business school graduation, though Kathy didn't speak to me during their visit, stomping in and out of my apartment with a pout on her pretty face. But they came. They were a few minutes late for our graduation march. Dad had never been late to anything of mine before. He wore a black turtleneck under his sport coat instead of his usual button-up shirt. Unwilling to acknowledge the vanities all of us have, not ready to acknowledge Dad as his own person, I thought he looked ridiculous. I wanted the Dad tailor-made for me.

When my grandmother moved from her home in Sun City, Arizona, to a retirement center nearby, I flew down to join Dad and my aunt Georgia and cousins who lived locally in helping her move. We put things in boxes and brought them to her apartment, helping her unpack, finding just the right place for her china cabinet, for the glass bells and birds she collected. Grandma, fiercely independent throughout her life, had been loath to leave her home, but her declining health required it. Dad and I stayed in twin beds in the guest room at her new facility. I seized the chance to talk to him one evening, as we sat opposite each other on faded bedspreads. The only light came from lamps on the bedside tables, which cast long shadows and left the corners of the room dark.

"You haven't been visiting," I said, intending to provoke. "I don't get it. When you come with Kathy, you guys don't show up until the day is half gone. Why don't you just let her finish her yoga on her own?"

He evaded my questions for a while, then snapped, "Don't you think it's hard being down here while you're here helping? People will say what a big help you are, and Kathy's going to be jealous. I will *not* let this marriage fail. You kids *will* see an example of a good marriage!"

I sat on the sagging mattress, staring at him, speechless for once, watching the electricity snap and pop in the frayed ends of a divorced family. So much said between his words: regret over a failed marriage he never saw coming; love for his wife; love for us kids; the value of family; his insecurities, tempered by his determination. We regarded each other with a mix of apprehension and wonder, each of us trying to comprehend the other's changing status and the resulting implications of affection and remove, independence and need. I wanted to hug him and say I loved him, say I was sorry we had talks like these, that I just needed to know that I was still important. The most I might have said was "okay" before we turned out our lamps and went to sleep. Or rolled over to stare into the dark.

Thinking back on it now, I craved the gentleness Dad had assumed with age and his new marriage, in part because it hadn't been as present when I was younger. Part of this gentleness came from the love he had for Kathy. I could see that, and appreciate it as a part of him, as something she gave to him in a way we kids could not. But my need for connection threatened Kathy because my relationship with her, very real in its own right, was made of different stuff. We both wanted my dad in different ways.

I didn't notice the point at which our roles changed places and I was the one checking on him, asking what they were taking with them when they were gone, how they were going to be safe. As Dad and Kathy headed into the wild, I worried, in the way we start to worry when we can no longer deny the possibility of loss, even though we have not yet begun to understand its consequences.

CHAPTER 4

DAMP SHADOWS

It is still beautiful to feel your heart throbbing.
But often the shadow feels more real than the body.

— Tomas Tranströmer, "After Someone's Death"

My first days back in Seattle after Dad and Kathy died had played out like a silent movie, familiar scenes and even people around me moving in two dimensions, black and white, muted, meaningless. I walked about as a void, a transparent body; no one could see me, no one could understand. I was living in negative. I lived just outside the tremulous border of life, on the fringe, the mirage of separation between worlds obscuring details and depth.

I fooled myself into believing that I could manage myself as a project. I did what must be done. We had a funeral. We buried them. We cleaned out and sold their house. If I planned well enough, my rational side could oversee my emotions. I went to a counselor and to a grief group. I returned to work and soon moved into management, where I dove into projects. I focused on rhythms: working, returning phone calls, seeing friends, going to church. I adopted two adolescent cats and named them Jack — after Father Jack, the priest in Healy who had buried Dad and Kathy, after the Jack River in Alaska, and after C. S. Lewis (Jack was Lewis's nickname) — and Healy, after the place where Dad and Kathy were buried. If life was about doing the right things, surely

I could figure those things out. This was something universal. Everyone loses their parents at some point.

But warning signs flashed like artillery fire in the night, unpredictable, shaking the ground, until I sat cowering, waiting for the next round to hit. I didn't feel my normal interest in the classical choral group I had sung with the previous year. I lacked motivation to reengage with much at all. In difficult times past, I had sat at my piano and let my fingers explore Chopin, Beethoven, searching for solace or companionship in music. Now I sat at the small dinner table in my apartment, moving food around on my plate in the smothering silence, glancing at the piano, mute against the far wall, feeling early autumn darkness bleed through the skylight above me and suffocate the light.

One night I pushed my plate away and stood. I walked to the piano and sat on the bench. I rested my hands on the cool, smooth keys. My hands would not move. I looked at them — quiet hands sitting on silent keys, as still as bones.

To anticipate the storms, I became a weatherman, reading the signs, looking for cues. If I couldn't change the weather, couldn't hold back the onslaught, maybe I could get out of the way. I wasn't very good at it. Water spouts erupted without warning in the midst of calm. One day at the office, I bolted up, closed the blinds, slammed the door, and sat back in my chair, turning to face the wall, weeping. The dam was weak; I could only try to respond to leaks.

When after the funeral an acquaintance recommended antidepressants, I was insulted. We were a family that didn't ask for help. We were tough. I believed this until the day, a few months after coming back to Seattle, when I sprinted out of the office and down the stairs to my car, hoping I wouldn't see anyone, my body convulsing before I could slam the car door behind me. I went to my therapy appointment that afternoon, dissolved in sobs for the first and only time during therapy, and asked for a prescription. I didn't go to therapy to cry; I went to therapy to work. The counselor seemed relieved by it all: the crying and the request. He wrote the prescription. I went home and looked at the pill in my palm. Round, white, like a baby aspirin. I didn't want to cancel out my feelings. I didn't want to stop feeling the pain that kept me closer to those I had lost. I wanted to hurt, but I also needed to work and live. Refusing to use an available tool didn't make sense. I waited a day, then another. Finally I added the little white pills to my vitamins and tried to ignore that I was using them. Over time, I started to understand that not asking for help was another legacy I could break. I started to see the damage done in our family that might have been avoided if we hadn't all been so proud. And that the way that damage had manifested was nothing to be proud of at all.

"Are you over it yet?" someone asked once.

"Have you moved on?" asked someone else.

I knew these were questions asked from a place of discomfort, by people who did not know, who didn't know what to say. Still, the queries came at me like blades. There is no such thing as getting over it, I wanted to scream, I wanted to whisper. There is no such thing as moving on, at least not how you've understood it before. It's like being tackled by something you hadn't known existed, then lying breathless on the ground, getting up slowly, and starting to walk again, alongside this thing, along with this thing. It's no wonder some stories describe the grim reaper as a person or thing hooded and unknown that shows up at our doors, takes up residence in our homes and lives and bodies, a thing dark and physical.

I had to learn to understand the world differently. I had to relearn the world, a world without my father, without my stepmother. Once I did this, I had to relearn myself without them too. It all looked flat, dimensionless, ugly. I did not know how to do this kind of learning. I did not want to learn this kind of life.

Dad said, coming back from his father's funeral, that he had somehow known as he carried the casket that he was carrying not his father but only his shell. I kept envisioning Dad and Kathy alone in boxes deep in the cold dark earth, now just flesh and bone.

Each day, I came home from work and stretched out on the couch, flattened like roadkill. I stared into the air hanging silent and dead, seeing nothing, waiting to be crushed under the weight of its emptiness. I did not want to talk to anyone, and yet I wished with desperation for someone who would be in that room with me, in that space, just sitting and breathing and giving life to the air. I wished for air that held the possibility of a call from Anchorage, Dad's voice on the phone, Kathy's laugh. If I thought at all, I thought in sharp shards of understanding that there were others around my city, around my world, also roiling under the weight of this dark, fathomless pain, and that knowledge was too much to bear.

I put on sunglasses to walk to the grocery store on a cloudy day. Inside, I avoided eye contact. The checkout attendant smiled brightly and asked how I was, a gesture I usually appreciated. I wrestled the corners of my closed mouth upward, briefly, in disbelief at the unknowing of the world. I signed my credit card receipt, dropped my sunglasses back onto my face, and walked out, back onto the street, where I was invisible. I wondered how anyone could be so cruel. I envied cultures that have mourning traditions, wearing black or rending garments. Then people would know; they would understand. Why had our culture done away with all that? To spare the majority the discomfort that each of us must one day face? And by doing so robbing every one of us of the space to grieve and neutering society's ability to mourn with the bereaved, our chance to appreciate life more for knowing death? I felt cheated. And it occurred to me that grief is something imposed, but that grieving is something that must be learned and, like anything of consequence, would reveal its realities slowly, over a lifetime. I had to learn it, so that I could make it through the shadowed valley and someday come out the other side. In my learning, I wanted to stay invisible — or if I had to be visible, to be left to my mourning. Lord, have mercy.

CHAPTER 5

THE RIVER WITHIN US

The river is within us.

−T. S. Eliot, "The Dry Salvages"

Stretching from the gentle braids of the river below us, octago-
nal shapes, seemingly endless, symmetrical and similar in size,
textured the tundra. The pattern looked as though a crystal had
multiplied out of control, spreading across the plain.

Wresting myself from my daze, I tried pushing myself toward
curiosity. "What are those shapes?" I asked through my headset,
pointing at the geometric forms. My voice echoed in the headset
as though I were speaking into a barrel.

"They're called polygons," Tom said, his pilot's crosscheck continuing seamlessly, looking into the sky, at the tundra below, at
the instruments, and back out again.

"How are they formed?"

"They say they're made out of ice. Not sure why they end up
all the same like that."

I looked at the uniformity, complexity, and scale of the tundra
polygons, amazed that there could be such naturally occurring
order. The structure soothed me, an architecture of earth and
water, a pattern of the land promising evidence of divine intention
in what I saw as chaos. I wanted to know the place I was coming
to for healing, hoping that learning more might help fill in the
void that had opened in my life a year ago, might answer questions
still unresolved.

Despite knowing of the influx of life to the Arctic in summer, looking down at the coastal plain did not yet inspire me to awe. To marvel over precariously balanced and prodigious life requires understanding, and my untrained eyes were not adequate to the task. I felt a flash of panic that I had lived too long away from wilderness ever to be able to truly appreciate this place. Skeins of river wove loosely back and forth on the tapestry of the tundra, braids voyaging through the landscape, returning to the main channel, venturing out again. Large gravel bars separated the river's threads. From above it looked as though someone had poured a can of paint over an angled canvas so that streams of color navigated their way over tiny inconsistencies to the end. The distance hid the details, simplified the journey.

What was I really doing here? Was I really here to finish their trip? Or was I reacting like a wild animal, facing off against a wild place that had taken my dad and Kathy? Where did I get the idea I had enough experience or aptitude to handle a trip on a river in the Arctic? What was I thinking?

I'd learned to skydive in college while reveling in the myth of immortality belonging only to the young. I most enjoyed relative work, the formations skydivers make in the sky during a jump. One of the most counterintuitive techniques in relative work is the way two skydivers dock, or connect, in the air. If the jumpers reach out to make the connection, their bodies skid across the sky away from each other. Skydivers have to fight the natural urge to reach for something, and instead pull their arms back, orienting themselves so that they move toward their partners' grasp. You have to trust. You have to let it happen.

I wasn't any good at applying the lessons of parachuting to life. Emotions were far more dangerous than relying on a small piece of nylon to deliver you from sky to earth. Real risk involves the heart.

Now I focused on the physical, looked at the river winding below. No matter how good our maps, they could not depict the

Hulahula River with a high degree of accuracy. In Arctic rivers, the force of water moves huge amounts of rock and sediment. Rivers begin flowing high at early melt, undercutting banks not only by their power but also because the moving water thaws the permafrost below. As the melting slows, so do the rivers, depositing their loads of sediment and glacial silt along the wide channels they cut when the rivers were higher. These deposits, from large rocks to the finest sand, form islands and change the contours of the shores. Over time, the entire path of a river can change as it crawls toward the sea. The power of water. The shifting of the earth.

When I was skydiving, I developed a ritual I observed on every plane ride in the minutes before hurling my body into the rushing wind: I said the Lord's Prayer. I prayed for those I loved. I prayed for forgiveness. I got someone to check my equipment. This time, I whispered the Lord's Prayer. I prayed for safety. And I remembered with a flash of pain and derision Kathy's last journal entry on June 23, her last written words: "Lord, keep us safe." I scowled out the window. It would be easier not to believe in God. It would be easier not to have to make sense of this. Maybe this place was too far north for prayer, too far north for hope.

"There are a couple of grizzlies," Tom noted casually. He banked the airplane hard toward the river, and I grabbed the handle above my head as g-forces pressed me against the seat. Below us, two large brown bears ran in long, loose bounds with a grace proportionate to their vigor. As with William Faulkner's Old Ben, they were "taintless and incorruptible." They were the wild in its truest form.

Over the past year, I had read anything I could find about bear, probing the dichotomy of my repulsion and wonder, trying to reconcile my horror and awe. The primal connection between human and bear fills volumes, most richly relayed in the oral traditions of indigenous peoples around the world who think of the bear, despite, and in part because of, its potential for danger, as perhaps the purest representative of true wilderness, a wilderness now relegated to the geographical borders of humanity but echoing through the millennia in our psyches.

Indigenous people found physical and behavioral resemblances between humans and bears: the bear's ability to walk upright, and his footprint, with the indentation of heel and arch, are among the clearest similarities. Bears are considered by scientists and indigenous alike to be highly intelligent and playful. Bears and humans both have omnivorous diets subject to change according to season, making the most of a fish run, a harvest of wild edibles, a deer kill, but typically consuming similar roots, berries, and plants.

Bears are also known for their maternal instincts, so much so that the medieval church used bear as symbol for the Virgin Mary. Mother bears disappear into dens to give birth to — to *bear* — blind, hairless, and helpless cubs weighing less than a pound, suckling them in the den, a second womb. Though the mother bear does not eat or drink during her winter sleep, her young grow to the point of viability before mother and young emerge in the spring. But unlike most other animals, a mother bear stays with her young for another two or three years, teaching them to forage, build dens, and avoid threats from larger bears. Like humans, each bear represents a considerable investment of maternal time and energy.

A bear carcass, killed and skinned, is purported to look eerily like a human corpse.

But how do I describe seeing a bear under my circumstances? I knew that bears generally stay clear of humans. I knew that the two bears below us had not killed Dad and Kathy, because that bear had been killed the next day, when the police went to recover their bodies. I knew that before (and after) Dad and Kathy were killed, there were no known bear killings in the Arctic Refuge. I knew that these bears were beautiful. I was riveted in wonder and in horror. A piece of me seized inside. I strained to hear a symphony, but my music crumbled into chaos. The patterns disappeared.

A memory: waking early in the morning in my upstairs room to hear Dad's quick, heavy footfalls on the first floor of the house moving from the bedroom to the kitchen, the sound of pouring coffee beans, the sound of coffee beans grinding, the sound of his footfalls returning to bed to wait while the coffee brewed, the smell of coffee curling through the house.

I depended on knowing. I knew facts. Facts were clean. They were neat and orderly, like the facts I'd researched and put on three-by-five cards when I debated in high school. Facts I could reference to prove a point, win an argument. I read about these bears the year after Dad and Kathy died. I continued to read about them. I knew them from the newspaper's picture of that seven-year-old, healthy grizzly on the north end of that Arctic beach, the remnants of the wrecked campsite just to the south.

Barren-ground grizzlies are smaller and more aggressive than their southern counterparts. Food on the Arctic tundra is scarce, and grizzlies, the brown bear with the least-dense population and the lowest reproductive rate, cover hundreds of square miles of territory to feed themselves and maintain their population. The barren-ground grizzly in the photo killed my father and stepmother. These were not clean facts. They dripped with gore.

The timbre of the Arctic's music changed. Red tooth and claw bristled on the clean lines of landscape. I knew the bears moved toward the river on the coastal plain where we would be in another week. Logically, they would have moved a distance away by the time we reached that point. And yet the existence of the grizzlies affirmed my entry into wilderness in the same inexplicable sense as seeing the polar bear in Kaktovik did; a surprising solace rested comfortably next to my abhorrence and just punctured the aridity of my spirit.

A memory: "If I die tomorrow," said Dad, many times, "I want you to remember that no matter how much money you make, you save at least ten percent of it, more if you can." That's not all I want to remember, Dad. But I remember. Ten percent.

Looking down to the coastal plain from the Cessna, I felt momentarily protected, and yet uncomfortably separate, from the wild world below. I was cocooned in the limits of my understanding, trying to squirm through what bound me, though my wings were yet unformed. I considered that when Faulkner's Ike went into the wild to see Old Ben, he left his weapon behind. Even that was not enough. He hung his compass and his watch on a tree. He left the trappings and security of his world behind to join the concert of wildness. I could not hang up my compass yet. "Be scared. You can't help that," Ike's mentor, Sam Fathers, said. "But don't be afraid." I was scared. And I was still afraid.

Along the west side of the river, we flew over two Inupiat fishing camps, shacks falling apart and old oil barrels askew on the tundra.

"See that hole?" Tom pointed out a gaping blackness in the side of one of the shacks. "That's where a grizzly forced its way in." I stared at the grotesque collision of ancient wisdom and ways of life, the violence of the wild, the violence of modernity, until it fell behind the plane's progress. Continuing south, the green coastal plain grew into foothills and the river disappeared into small canyons. Held in by the high and narrow banks, the river leapt and churned.

"Those are the rapids?" I asked Tom through the headset. "They don't look too bad."

"They're not—from up here," he said, smiling.

A memory: running with Dad over his lunchtimes the summer I was ten years old and entering my first 10k races with him. "See that guy ahead of you in the red shorts?" Dad asked, as we started up a hill. "He's slowing down where it gets steep. Let's pass him!"

Despite my Alaskan upbringing, I'd never seen this landscape over which we flew, a landscape unknown even to most Alaskans because of its inaccessibility. Westerners are new to this land, but people have lived in the northernmost reaches of Alaska for more than ten thousand years. The Inupiat populate the coastal areas. The Gwich'in Indians live south of the Brooks Range in a region stretching from central Alaska into Canada. Both depend on the land and the sea to sustain their communities, even today. For the Gwich'in, reliant on the Porcupine Caribou Herd, the Arctic Coastal Plain is known as "the place where life begins" and as "the sacred calving grounds." Neither people is constrained by state or country borders, a reminder that the wilderness is bigger than any more recent attempts to define it.

Russians and Europeans were the first Westerners to explore Arctic Alaska, beginning with Captain Cook mapping its coastline in 1778. The search for the Northwest Passage brought back news of whales, beginning decades of aggressive whale hunting. Most whaling expeditions lasted two years, sailing around the coast of South America, whaling and offloading the oil and baleen in the Hawaiian Islands (and frequently picking up Hawaiians to help crew), then continuing north to the Arctic until winter forced the ships south again.

The name Hulahula is first noted in correspondence between S. J. Marsh, a prospector at the turn of the twentieth century, and Alfred H. Brooks, chief geologist for the U.S. Geological Survey in the same period in a paper dated 1919. The river was referred to as "Hoolahoola," a word of Kanaka, or Hawaiian, origin, meaning "the dance." The paper notes that there was no ancient name for the river, and that "Hoolahoola" was bestowed in the past twenty years (since 1900) after natives of Herschel Island, a tiny island in the Beaufort Sea just off the coast of Canada's Yukon Territory, killed a number of caribou and celebrated with a dance by the river. It is not known how the name was given or why a name of Hawaiian origin was chosen. Perhaps a crew member from the islands suggested it. But the name stuck. The dance. A celebration.

Whaling continued until several factors brought it to a halt, among which were the last shots of the Civil War, fired by the Confederate ship *Shenandoah* in the Bering Strait on June 22, 1865. Though it was two months after Lee's surrender, the *Shenandoah* hadn't got the word. It burned twenty-one Arctic whalers in this two-month period, decimating the whaling fleet. The *Shenandoah* learned the war was over in August when it arrived on the California coast. Whaling gave way to walrus hunting, which continued until restrictions were imposed in the midtwentieth century.

The Cold War military buildup increased the number of visitors to the Arctic, along with the establishment of the Distant Early Warning Line, a series of communications stations intended to provide warning of Soviet attack. The subsequent discovery of oil led to increased development and debate, with worldwide interest from oil companies looking for extraction opportunities and environmentalists defending the uniqueness and fragility of the Arctic ecosystem.

Both Dad and Kathy had been in Alaska since the late 1960s. Today's literature describes the experience of that decade with talk of protests, drugs, and sex, but Dad felt a sense of honor in entering the army on the draft after completing law school. He trained as an enlisted combat engineer before realizing that his law degree allowed him the opportunity for service as an army attorney in the Judge Advocate General's Corps. Though initially he was slated for Vietnam, the army sent him to Alaska, flying him around the state executing wills and powers of attorney and prosecuting the myriad drug cases defining military JAG at the time. When his military commitment ended, a year after I was born, he worked in Anchorage for the city attorney's office and then opened a private practice. He fell in love with the land and, for as long as I can remember, pulled us along with him on backpacking trips in the Chugach Mountains, and even on a few easy river trips by canoe.

Kathy came to Alaska after a construction job in West Africa. Her adventurous spirit was unquenched by her sorority days at Depauw and a subsequent master's in education at the University of Texas. She brought her bright blue eyes and full, sweet laugh to Denali National Park to work as a naturalist when the roads were still closed all winter and only a weekly train brought supplies or the opportunity to head into town. She was one of those women a lot of men are secretly in love with. Kathy taught at Tri-Valley Elementary School a few miles north of Denali fall through spring. She traveled with her first husband, a wildlife photographer, by foot and folding kayak around the interior of Alaska. After their divorce, she taught in Anchorage, settling into a city routine. She and Dad married with the agreement that he would learn to dance and she would learn to ski. They compromised by doing neither. Still, when Dad started turning more attention to the outdoors after years of office sequestration, it was not a new experience for her.

They began longer river trips in the late 1990s. Their river journal from 1999 begins with a recipe for raisin muffins, and then: "Banks of the Yukon. Just entering dozen islands." One journal records trips on the Tanana in 1999, the Charley River in 2000, Harriman Fjord in 2000, and the Gulkana River in 2001. Dad's enthusiasm was initially too much; on the trip down the Charley River in the interior of Alaska, Kathy's kayak flipped, and her head — luckily helmeted — hit a rock. They pulled over. She was spooked and angry. One day into the trip, they made camp on a gravel bar, which was as far as they traveled. They contacted the one plane flying over their area each day with their VHF radio and arranged for an early pickup.

Dad learned from that experience. After a safe return, they took two trips to the weeklong Otter Bar Kayak School in California, spent evenings on rivers at home, and built back up to remote passages. Kathy was less interested in whitewater than she was in time with her husband, so Dad was happy to hike back and paddle her boat through areas where she was uncomfortable. They kayaked the Canning River on the far west boundary of the Arctic National Wildlife Refuge in 2004. The Hulahula River is the next navigable drainage to the east. I imagine Dad had in mind traveling each of the rivers in the refuge in the same way he had read his way chronologically through American literature, starting with the sermons of Cotton Mather. Once the magic of the Arctic worked its way under his skin, it became a part of him, that much I knew.

Now I embarked to find my father, to know him, having realized, once he was gone, how little I knew of him, unwilling to accept that what I knew of my father was all I would have a chance to know. I hoped for just a glimpse of some of the magic I knew he and Kathy had experienced on this trip. Throughout humankind's long history, the idea of journey has carried with it expectations of adventure, of wildlife, of challenge, of conquest. I was scared to have any expectations, no longer knowing how to consider this thing called life after the past summer. I stared out of the Cessna's windows. Farther upriver, thin blue and white lines of *aufeis* began to define the riverbanks of the river valley.

Aufeis was one thing I had been concerned about on the river. It forms in winter months, when water flowing in a deeper channel of the river is dammed by an ice jam downriver in a shallower channel. The water continues to flow beneath the dam, but also overflows it, spreads out over the banks, and freezes. This cycle of overflowing and freezing happens many times, until the ice forms up to three meters deep. Until the spring melt, this thick ice stretches across the river, but water still flows beneath it, and the current can sweep boats beneath the ice, resulting in capsizing and drowning. This year, the aufeis had melted from the channel. It didn't look like we would have a problem.

The greatest danger I felt then, and sometimes still feel, is of losing the memories.

When Dad and Kathy had flown in last year, it had been colder, with aufeis choking the river. They were excited to be heading back into the wilderness. Later, Tom told reporters that Kathy had questioned him thoroughly about emergency procedures. I remembered reading the newspaper article. I remembered walking into the silent house. I remembered dinner at Sostanza in Seattle with them both, the fireplace warming the room. I remembered so much, and so little. Time's linearity evaporated as we flew against the river's current below. Was I trespassing too much among the bones of the dead? Qarrtsiluni. Have mercy.

Foothills drawn in the muted browns, greens, and ochre of sandstone and limestone grew into the heights of the Romanzof Mountains, and the glacial peaks of Michelson and Chamberlin soared to either side. Valleys leading back into mountains beckoned me. Farther south, the river spread out again as the valley widened, no longer confined to the canyons. The sweep of land appeared more desolate than life-giving. *"Yea, though I walk through the valley of the shadow of death."* What was I thinking? This couldn't be a good idea.

A tundra airstrip came into focus on the west side of the river — Grasser's, one of the more established landing areas in the Arctic, named for Marlin Grasser, who spent time on the Hulahula River in the mid- and late-twentieth century, guiding sheep hunters. Tom flew over, banked for a steep approach, and landed the airplane. He killed the engine. We jumped out. Ned and Sally had been standing at the edge of the airstrip; now they joined us, and the four of us rapidly unloaded the remaining bags from the back of the plane.

There is a saying in Alaska that three things kill small-plane pilots: weather, weather, and weather. With clouds likely to close in, Tom wasn't taking any chances. By the time we pulled the gear to the side of the landing strip, he had cranked the propeller and maneuvered the 206 for takeoff. With a burst of noise, the Cessna rolled down the strip on fat tundra tires, and wings grabbed air. The buzz of the plane dissolved to the north. Except for a light breeze, it was quiet.

CHAPTER 6

LIVE WATER

Live water heals memories.
— Annie Dillard, *Pilgrim at Tinker Creek*

Ned and Sally had already sorted the gear and inflated the large blue raft by the time I arrived. Mountains of limestone, sandstone, and shale framed our embarkation point, ancient rocks deposited by ancient seas forced upward by the pressure of the Pacific Plate far to the south. These mountains were the second range pushed up by tectonic forces; the first range had eroded away, and the newer mountains continue to reach skyward even today. The sprawling scape was a picture of the oldest forces of creation, a valley carved by glacier, water, and wind, the rise and fall of oceans, the shaping of a world long before our time.

Relative to the geologic context, the pile of gear that had seemed so immense as we loaded the Cessna shrank, along with us, to insignificance. We had departed with much, but it was contained for river travel in bear-proof food canisters and waterproof dry bags we had packed before leaving for the airplane. Before the trip, the food we needed for ten days had spread out to cover the floor and furniture of the living room in the Denali cabin from which we had launched our expedition. I had counted out packets of oatmeal, candy bars, energy bars, dehydrated food. With permanent marker and duct tape, we had labeled the bear canisters with the number of days worth of meals they contained.

We didn't talk about the other load, the one there was no manual for securing. Memories, fear, horror, determination, unworthiness, emptiness. I didn't begin to know how to secure these things, or how to let them go.

"You guys ready for this?" Sally asked.

"Sure." I smiled.

How would I survive this?

Ned started cinching down straps on each side of the boat. He seemed to measure the strap tension with his eyes, repositioning dry bags as needed, yanking on the ends of the straps until they were tight enough to strain against the rough rope running around the top of the raft.

"What about you?" I asked.

"Heck yeah!" Sally said. "This is going to be great!"

"We got a nice day to start, at least," I said, trying to swallow my unease.

The two guns were also in dry bags. I was uncomfortable with their positioning. Eight years of military training had drilled into me the importance of safety; barrels of loaded weapons are always pointed up and away from people, but cramming them in a raft didn't permit the same level of discipline. Despite our best efforts, our discipline was far from military.

We finished packing the raft. Each dry bag had its place, and canvas compression straps secured the load onto the fourteen-foot blue rubber craft. Ned tightened each strap one final time with easy confidence and a force approaching viciousness. The side of the raft read NRS, the brand; I thought for this journey she should have a name. *Hope*, perhaps. Or *Desperation*. *Longing*, maybe. *Prayer*, even better. Or *Stupidity*. I tried to put these thoughts out of my mind. I clipped my daypack close to me with a carabiner on a compression strap, being careful not to let my most precious cargo — the small plastic bottle and the plastic bag I had transported carefully from Seattle, along with a tiny silver amulet from Father Jack in Healy — be crushed by other gear or the boat.

Kathy's journal entry on their first day was this:

6-15-05 7:08 PM ... Beautiful flight up river and landed at gravel bar airstrip. Within 2 hours saw a wolf and about 20 dall sheep, ewes and lambs.... there's a strong wind from the north which makes for lots of layers of clothing. But the sun is shining and ... we are thrilled to be back in God's country again! Keep us safe, Lord. Kathy

"Let's get this in the water," Ned said. "Can you each grab a side?" Sally and I took positions on either side and grabbed the rope. "One, two, pull!" Ned said. The raft followed us reluctantly to rest on the water.

Dad and Kathy had pitched a tent at Grasser's and stayed to relax and hike for a day, but we wanted to get some water under us, to accept the river's invitation, to move forward. The sun glanced off the surface of the water, and a light breeze cooled our skin. I inhaled deeply, and exhaled, slowly. We were doing it. After the frigidity of the coast, I relaxed into the warmth of the sun.

I sat on the port side of the raft, feigning confidence, worried that our steed would feel my inexperience, sense my trepidation. But if she did, she didn't show it. My seat felt secure, and my paddle strokes against the water smooth. It occurred to me I wanted too much from this trip. For those of us who spend less time in wild places than we do in cities, it's easy to arrive with urban expectations, with checklists of hopes and desires. This is the wrong way to come into a wilderness bigger than any of the demands that can be made of it. Lessons and healing come only through an open spirit and uncluttered mind. I felt poorly positioned for success.

Though VHF and UHF radios and a satellite phone stayed handy in waterproof bags, we couldn't have been farther from any reality outside of wilderness. With the exception of a handful of other adventurers making their way on this or other Arctic rivers and the three hundred people in the village of Kaktovik, there were no other people within hundreds of square miles. Despite the relative explosion in adventure travel and ecotourism, not to mention continued hunting in the Arctic, only a few hundred people visit the Arctic Refuge each year.

The freezing-cold glacial water moved beneath us. I watched the etchings of currents hinting at complexity beneath the otherwise smooth surface. It was secret water, shadow water, dream water. And it was wild water, birthed in the mountains, running to the sea. It lived. It breathed. "Live water heals memories," says Annie Dillard. It seemed to me that this water threatened to open them back up.

"Sheep in the mountains," Ned commented.

Far to the east, thirty or more Dall sheep drifted slowly across the mountainside. I smiled slightly, almost against my will. I craved beauty; I wasn't ready for beauty. Were they the same flock Dad and Kathy had seen last year on arriving at Grasser's?

The river flowed here between limestone mountains on both sides, austere rock with wide valleys and steep cuts. Utter wildness and immensity surrounded me. But a sticky web of determination, horror, fear, exhilaration, and desperation held me fast, even as the river ran freely. I considered that we safeguard our fears more closely than our joy. I came here city-soft, and flabby, in spirit and body.

The summer sun was unexpectedly warm, but the weather shifted fluidly. I wore an old dry suit on loan from Sally. It was made of a heavy nylon incapable of breathing and had thick rubber funnels at the neck and wrists to keep out icy water. I alternately sweated and froze.

The mountains soared on either side. The river was open here, though not deep. Each paddle stroke loosened my joints and my mind, and at some point I didn't recognize, I felt the rhythm of my paddle and the rhythm of the land. Our journey moved forward as smoothly as the river's surface, but we were an alien presence in this wild, open space burdened and freed by the emptiness that stretched and settled with threat and promise. Although I'd hoped that Dad and Kathy's journal, their exploration, would guide me on this trip, hoped that if my body traversed similar paths, perhaps my spirit would find them still here somehow, so far it seemed I saw only shadow.

Sally started out as captain, sitting at the stern and steering. Ned and I sat on either side forward on the raft.

"So the captain gives the commands on the boat," Ned explained. "And the people in front execute on those commands."

"We can practice," Sally said. "I'll give the command 'Paddle right!' and the person on the right paddles forward. Or 'Paddle right, back-paddle left!' if we really need to make a hard turn."

"What else do we need to know to read the river?" I asked. I knew some of what would follow from having taken kayaking courses in western North Carolina years earlier, but I was not too proud for a refresher from people proficient in the sport.

"The big thing to pay attention to is the difference between a hole and a rock," Ned said. "Think of it like a smiley face or a frowny face. See how the water over there to the left pours over and it looks like a frown?"

"Sure," I said.

"That's a hole. If it's big enough and you don't take it correctly, it can push a boat to the bottom and hold you there."

"Doesn't sound like a good idea."

"I don't think there's anything on this river big enough to do that," Ned said, "but it's something to pay attention to."

"Great. And what about the rocks?"

The banks moved behind us smoothly. Beyond us, the mountains seemed to recline, gentle and firm.

"Paddle both," Sally said. Ned and I took several strokes, gaining speed in a shallow section. The rocks below scraped the bottom of the boat, but our momentum propelled us forward.

"See how the water moves around that rock about one o'clock?" Ned said.

"Yes."

"You can see the rock protruding from the water, and the water is going around it, like a smiley face," Ned said.

"So that's good?"

"Well, you can see where it is. Really, by itself it isn't a problem. If you hit it, you'll bounce off of it. You just have to be careful if there are several of them, or if there's a hole in front of it."

"Paddle right, five strokes," Sally said. I took five strong strokes and the raft moved left, skirting the rock Ned had pointed out.

"Anything else?"

"You need to be able to read where the current is and what it's doing," Ned said. "So look ahead. Can you tell where the water's going?"

A strong current curved gently toward the right bank, and tiny ripples indicated a gravel bar on the left. "Toward the right."

"Exactly," Ned said. "We want to stay in the current as much as we can, but it will take us into the bank if it's strong enough, so you have to start paddling away from the bank before you get all the way there to stay in the current."

We scraped the rocky bottom several times, and the heavy raft proved unwieldy in the shallow water. But the river here was a single channel, and the path of the current was clear.

"Whoa, watch out!" Sally yelled.

I twisted around on my seat to see an Arctic tern streaking from the sky toward us, black-hooded head on a lean, white body with forked tail and tapered wings. It dove straight at the boat, its screech following its tail feathers as it pulled up and away just before impact.

"She must have a nest around here. Paddle forward!"

The tern swooped again, pulling up just inches from us.

"Keep paddling!" Strong paddle strokes forward, a third surgical swoop, and she arced gracefully away.

I took a deep breath. "That was a little unnerving."

"No joke," Sally said.

I glanced back nervously to be sure the tern wasn't following us. Its screaming descents echoed inside of me like a warning, a prophecy I wasn't equipped to understand. The sudden violence of its appearance sheared away any pretense of comfort. Then again, perhaps it was a blessing. Nowhere is it guaranteed that a blessing comes with comfort. I had quit my tent and come here for God; maybe I wasn't prepared for what he would say or how he would say it. Maybe I wasn't prepared for what he would not say.

Instead of fear, I should have found inspiration: the Arctic tern's endurance and tenacity are legendary. Like most birds that come to the Arctic to nest and bear young, the Arctic tern chases the sun to the Antarctic every winter, making the global journey again the next summer. Perhaps in anticipation of life's demands, chicks are born with eyes open and covered in protective down, able to move about, an adaptation classifying them as precocial and giving them a head start on survival. Tough and enduring. I didn't feel tough. I would need to find a way to endure.

Save for the Arctic tern, the day was full of bouncy wave trains and "rock gardens," mazes of exposed rocks in shallow sections of the river. I acknowledged my pleasure with reluctance, but I couldn't help laughing at the bounce of the boat, smiling — even, for just a while, grinning.

Halfway through the day, after we pulled over for a quick snack, Sally said, "Why don't you try the captain's position?"

"Really?" I asked. "I haven't done this river stuff as much as you guys."

"You'll do fine," she said. "Don't you think, Ned?"

"You'll do fine. Try it and see if you like it," he said.

I took the captain's seat at the stern. Despite my inexperience, our new arrangement worked well, as Ned and Sally could anticipate the requirements of the river from the bow. I liked having the back of the raft to myself with space and time and quiet to think.

"How's that look to the right for a campsite?" I asked, as evening approached with only the slightest dimming of daylight. I did a strong back-paddle on the right side. The raft swung toward the bank. I looked for the eddy, where the current curled back on itself after a small protrusion of land, resting on its journey. "Paddle forward!" Ned and Sally pulled with their paddles, and when the water was shallow enough, Sally jumped out and grabbed the rope to pull the raft onto the shore. The three of us hauled the raft well up and out of the water. It moved easily with the water's support.

On their first day on the river, Dad wrote in his journal that it had been windy and cold, and they'd had to go a long way to find their first campsite because of the aufeis. Still, in his entries, the excitement of the journey is palpable. I found myself reading and rereading his simple notes, just so I could look for a connection, so I could imagine their joy, so I could imagine them alive.

6/17/05 Wind continued all night & fog to the ground after 2:00 AM. By 7:30 it lifted and signs of blue sky but cold strong wind from the north.... It's nice to be on the water — a pretty little river with a lot of bounce! Shallow and braided in many areas. We saw many sheep and groups of 35! Stopped at Potok.... The wind made going very slow & cold in the face. We camped at a bar at 4:00 and had a really nice dinner ... to bed by 8:30. A really nice day for us both. Rich

Kathy spotted a pure white wolf — huge about 1/4 mile away running on the slope. He would lope, then stop and look at us — really something ... Some rock faces started appearing and then the wind really came back in force. (I forgot to mention we got out earlier at East Potuk Creek — another landing area — pretty neat.) At Koloktuk Creek there was an extended rock garden. We both got high ended and Kathy couldn't get off so I threw a rope and pulled her off. This led to a pretty neat rapids with a lot of rocks to dodge and then a right turn and a drop at the end. Kathy decided not to paddle so I paddled both boats. The boats with the load and the wind don't maneuver so well. We began looking for camp spots and were immediately in aufeis on both sides and no campsites for a long way. The excitement of the day was a very big collapse of an ice shelf adjacent to me—it created a sudden large wave which flipped me over. Kind of fun but a big surprise. We always try to keep our distance but the wind was driving us into the ice much closer than normal—maybe 30'. Kathy saw it all ... she said a 3' wave. The rest of the day was tough. The clouds kept building, wind I would guess was 40 MPH in our face. Water kept whipping up all over us. It was tough to stay in any channel. We wound up lining boats a fair distance. Finally we found a sand bar that would work and we set up camp about 5:00. We think we may start leaving earlier to avoid the inevitable and unrelenting cold north wind that picks up later in the day ... Rich.

I was glad we hadn't faced similar winds or aufeis so far. It was hard thinking of Dad and Kathy out on this river, fighting the wind. It was harder thinking of them having been on the river, and then no longer being. This journal entry was Father's Day, the day I had talked to them on the sat phone.

The three of us walked the tundra around our chosen campsite, looking for bear sign and for areas to set up the tents and the kitchen. I automatically recalled my military training, a posture of aggression and defense that felt both natural and unwelcome. I looked for clear fields of fire, lines of sight. Open tundra rolled away from our campsite for a mile or more before reaching the base of the mountains, and the low mosses, sedges, and lichens allowed visibility that satisfied both wilderness and military requirements.

We made our kitchen two hundred yards north of the boat and

close to the river. The kitchen is where we would store the food and all the cooking and personal hygiene items. When camping in bear country, anything that has a fragrance must be stored well away from the tent, because it can attract bears. We knew that we had far more gear than we needed — several stoves, water filters, and tents, in case anything broke down, clogged, or tore. Fortunately, heavier loads are easier to manage in a raft than in a backpack. Sally brought a bivvy sack and a large mesh tent, anticipating the mosquitoes. Ned brought two smaller mountaineering tents. I brought a tarp. The redundancy, even if excessive, offered all of us a sense of security.

Of the many suggestions to mitigate risk that percolated among the guiding community after last year's attack, one was that sleeping in a floorless tent might help afford visibility and preclude entanglement in the tent fabric. That's why I'd brought a tarp; it would provide shelter, visibility, and, if needed, mobility. But as I attempted to set it up, the wind ripped the thin material out of my hands. Annoyed with myself, I borrowed one of the two tents Ned had brought with him.

We also set up a bear fence around our sleeping area, a set of thin electric wires on stakes and a small battery-powered energizer. Bear fences were first developed in New Zealand to control sheep. Some outdoors outfitters used them to protect food stashes or even bush planes. The fence was intended to shock and thus deter a curious animal. Dad and Kathy had traveled with a bear fence on the Canning River, but had not brought one with them on the Hulahula. I was far from convinced of its efficacy. Sally and I began to set up our camping gear. I pulled out the collapsible tent poles and assembled them before threading them through the sleeves of the tent.

"I'm sure people would think we're overreacting, setting a bear watch, on top of having a bear fence, guns, and bear spray," I said. I blew into the small valve of my sleeping pad to inflate it, soon feeling light-headed from the attempt.

"Well, the bear watch is fine with me," Sally said.

"I doubt that anyone else does it or would even recommend it," I said. "It just seems like a good idea, given everything. Our family back home will be more comfortable. Maybe it will even be nice, having a few quiet hours alone at night."

Ned said nothing, finally clipping the last wire of the bear fence into place and connecting it to the ground and energizer. He pushed the power button, and the quiet but persistent high-pitched beeping, assuring the user of its operation, began.

"Works," he said, his voice flat. Ned wasn't engaging, at least on the surface. From experience, I knew this meant he was holding things in. It had been so long since I had seen him that I no longer knew how to expect his reticence to manifest. On a family trip in college once, he'd lunged at me from the guest bedroom he shared with Sam when I came in to get my roller bag; afterward Dad pinned him against the wall to make the point that he was not to physically threaten anyone in our family. Later, Dad was overcome by emotion. It was one of two times I'd seen him cry, the first when he and our mom had told us they were divorcing. "I shouldn't have confronted him like that," he said. "I shouldn't have challenged his manhood."

"Really, Dad? Instead, you'd just let him threaten the women in this family?"

Of course Dad wouldn't let that happen; he was the force moderating Ned's anger and physical threats, whether they were directed against my mom, Kathy, or me.

But that had been more than a decade ago. People grow up, I thought. Young men become men, don't they?

I gave Ned a quick hard look, then looked away.

As the three of us walked to the kitchen site, I rested the shotgun on my shoulder.

Λ

The decision to bring weapons had not come easily. Since the Inuit always travel with high-caliber weapons in the Arctic, it seemed a good idea. Still, many naturalists and other adventurers do not believe in bringing weapons into the wilderness. And I couldn't help thinking of Faulkner's Ike leaving his gun behind.

A month before departing for the Arctic, I'd met my younger brother, Sam, off I-5 halfway between Portland and Seattle to pick up Dad's two guns, which Sam had stored at his house in Oregon. He handed me the long black plastic cases in a fast-food parking lot. I placed them carefully in my trunk. The gravity of transferring firearms weighted the cases even more. It felt like an illicit activity. It also felt like the first real step toward the Arctic trip.

I also knew how important it was to be comfortable using them. My good friend and running partner Trea, a marine, agreed to go with me to an indoor range before the trip. Inside the one-story, warehouse-style building, well-maintained weapons hung on the walls and neatly stacked boxes of ammunition sat on shelves. We each carried a gun case.

The manager, a middle-aged man in jeans and an untucked plaid shirt with a knife case attached to his belt, didn't try to suppress his amusement at two women coming through the door. We laid the cases on the counter.

"What do you have there?" he asked.

"45-70 Copilot and a pistol-grip shotgun," I said, feigning confidence and suppressing a laugh at the clash of what I'd come to understand as city life in Seattle and large caliber weaponry.

The manager raised his eyebrows. "What you gonna do with those?" The condescension disappeared from his voice.

"Protection from bear in Alaska," I said.

"So you'll be using slugs in the shotgun, right?"

I nodded.

"Slugs are too big for this range," he said, then hesitated for a minute. "Come on back." He grabbed headphones and ammunition.

We followed hopefully into the narrow hallway of firing lanes smelling of gunpowder and metal.

"Okay, you ever shot this before?" he asked, sighting down the barrel of the 45-70.

"No, but we've both shot other rifles—M16s, M60s," I said.

His eyebrows raised again, then relaxed into a smile. "Who woulda guessed? Okay, well, this is gonna kick a lot more than those. See, those have recoil built into them. These don't. You want to really jam it into your shoulder, like this," he demonstrated, pulling the butt of the rifle firmly into the pocket where his shoulder connected to his arm. "And you know you don't want to anticipate the shot. Just take it from there."

He dropped a cartridge into the chamber, moved the lever down and back to the stock, sighted down the barrel easily, and fired. A paper target down the lane took his shot dead center. He handed me the rifle. I pulled the heavy wooden stock into my shoulder. Breathe-relax-aim-squeeze-shoot. Wait for the pause after you exhale to pull the trigger. My training flowed easily back, and the stock slammed into my body. I concentrated on the target. Breathe-relax-aim-squeeze-shoot and *wham!* Another slam into my shoulder.

Trea and I both shot and hit pretty close to center mass.

"Not bad!" he said with a smile. "Shotgun?" He picked up the heavy metal gun. "You ready to hit a bear with one of these things?" he asked.

"Hopefully we won't have to," I said, parroting what I knew I should say. "It would be rare. They generally stay away from people and usually don't cause any trouble. I really don't want to have to shoot at anything." As I said it, I believed it, or most of me did, and yet I realized how ludicrous it would sound to anyone who knew what had happened last year.

The manager nodded. "Well, don't tell anyone," he said. "We're not really supposed to do this, but here's slugs, here's the shot. You gonna carry this, you need to be ready to shoot it."

The pistol-grip shotgun had an eighteen-inch barrel, the shortest legal length. It had been a gift to Dad from his friend George in the army. George and his sons were hunters, and this was widely considered a standard bear gun in Alaska.

I tried it first. The gun weighed heavy in my arms, requiring commitment and intention. Holding the pump and the pistol grip, I aimed at the target. The percussion echoed down the lane. My shot demolished the top quarter of the paper target.

"You've got to aim it lower than you think," the manager said. "You'll naturally pull up, so get it lower." I tried again. Center mass, a huge hole ripped from the target. Trea followed suit, hitting center mass on her first try. The explosions reverberated in the emptiness inside me.

A bolt. A bullet. A chamber. The 45-70 had been found lying next to Dad on the sands of that Arctic beach. He had actioned the lever, but never had the chance to fire. The gun was the last thing he had touched.

Λ

Years before, I'd visited my grandma in Phoenix. Before I left, she asked how my brothers were doing.

"Fine, I think, Grandma," I said. "They're boys. They don't say much."

"Last time Ned was here," she said, "I took him to the airport when he left. He gave the agent his ticket, and as he started to walk down the jetway, I said, 'Keep the faith, Ned!' He turned around and yelled back at me, 'No!' And then he kept going." She shook her head slowly. "I just hope he's okay."

"I don't know, Grandma. We don't really talk about those things."

I remembered that conversation as Ned, Sally, and I each took care of our gear, getting ready for the night. Ned was so sensitive that he couldn't take the tiniest disruption, arming himself with anger for protection. I didn't remember him that way in child-hood, only since our parents' divorce, though I supposed he had experienced additional stresses as an adopted sibling that I would never understand. I watched the care he took with everything, appreciating his attention to detail, worrying about the precision he seemed to demand and what might fail to live up to his expecta-tions on this trip. I shook off the thought and headed to my tent. Not something I could solve. I had my own problems.

Sally took the first shift to watch for bear. I had the second. I wiggled into my sleeping bag, wadding up my raincoat for a pillow and pulling a T-shirt over my eyes to keep out the light.

At 11:00 p.m. I awoke to Sally's tapping on the nylon vesti-bule of my tent, waking me for bear watch. The tapping came thin and soft, a reminder of how little stood between me and this wilderness.

I crawled out of my tent into the middle of a watercolor paint-ing, the water, tinted and glistening, still moist on the paper. The brightness of the Arctic summer sun had lessened as the sun swung closer to the horizon, letting soft shadows from the west stretch gently across the tundra, and the watery light of rain showers in the mountains smoothed the edges of the limestone and shale while illuminating the mountainsides with a yellow glow. As the wind died, I shed my clothing down to my long under-wear, though the quick clustering of mosquitoes forced me just as quickly back into my rain gear and a mosquito head net. Resting the shotgun against a piece of driftwood, I sat with the journal, a book of Mary Oliver poetry, and the oversized can of bear spray and let the landscape saturate my eyes and soul.

This was our first night on the river. One year ago exactly, it had been Dad and Kathy's last night on earth. The pain of the past year returned like the twisting of a blade.

One night at home in my Seattle apartment, only weeks after returning from Alaska, I sat on the overstuffed denim couch, tucked under a quilt, reading. I looked up from my book — my concentration was so poor! — and my eye caught the leather brief-case of Dad's I had placed under the coffee table. I put my book down carefully. I slid down to sit on the floor and pulled the briefcase toward me. The thick brown leather bore scratches and dents from decades of use, the brass latch marred from years of protecting and releasing its contents. Inside were the newspaper articles from the summer, the funeral service bulletins, sympathy cards, death certificates. I looked over the articles, which still didn't register to me as real. Then the crisp blue-and-white death certificate, with the raised imprint of the coroner. "Cause of death: 1. Massive blunt force injuries, 2. Bear mauling." Did the coroner write this same thing after every bear attack? Or had he really done an examination?

In the back of the briefcase was a manila envelope, taped shut. I replaced the articles, the bulletin, the certificate. I pulled out the envelope.

One corner of the envelope was creased into a fold. I smoothed it back with my thumb, as though I could flatten it, make it right. Then, with some masochistic sense of resolve, I slid my finger under the flap of the envelope and tore it open. The unedited police report slid out, a neat stapled packet. I read through each page, slowly. My stomach tightened. Bile rose in my throat. The mirage that is our days and hours evaporated, hurling me back to the phone call, to a gruesome event I'd only imagined and now understood through the detailed report of its aftermath. The report described me as having blond hair and green eyes, and said I was several years older than I was and living in Oregon. I was momentarily angered by this misidentification and then amused, as though my neurons no longer knew how to react. And then, reading further, I was offended: Dad and Kathy were bodies. The body of a man. The body of a woman.

I read the report like an addict who had abstained too long and now pushed the needle into her vein.

I should have recognized the signal, should have understood what it meant: I was whirling in the winds of the vortex still, believing in the power of information. Still believing that I could change the outcome.

I clutched at the couch with one hand. With the other I dug my fingers into my rib cage as though to keep my body from spinning apart. I rolled onto my side. The harsh light of the reading lamp's bare bulb shone into my pupils, but all I could see was darkness, dimensionless, interminable, and terrifying. I lay curled and helpless, focusing on how to take each breath, my arms clutching my sides with tightly curled fingers as though only the tension in my body could hold my life in one piece. Any doubts I may have had about the effect that violence in our souls has on our bodies evaporated in the pain of clarity.

I blinked to force my senses to readjust to the scene, the soft gurgle of the current against the shore, the light soft on the mountains. I was on the river where they'd made their final journey. It was my last attempt at understanding. I whispered aloud, to God, to the bears, to Dad. "Come on, bears, give us a break out here, won't you?" I was scared, in part because of the bears, but also because the nightmare that everyone has who loses a loved one was coming true: I had a hard time remembering Dad, the specifics of his face and his voice. And worse: I couldn't stop thinking about the image of him and Kathy screaming in a tent being ripped down around them. I prayed to understand, and I prayed for help — what kind of understanding or what kind of help, I'm not sure I knew, or know even now. "Help me, God. Help me, God," was all I could say. And then: "Come on, Dad. Can you show yourself, just for a minute? Come say hi? Come give me a hug?" Some small part of me thought maybe he was here. That he and Kathy would walk up with smiles on their faces and everything would be okay. The breeze carried my whispers off and away along the lines of the landscape.

An hour after midnight, the sun swung behind the mountains, but did not set. It would not set at all this far north and this close to solstice. Its low angle bathed the tundra and the mountains on either side in lambent yellow light. Gray tendrils of rain washed detail from ridgelines. Golden light shimmering on water suspended in the air soaked the land in an ethereal luminance. The muted glow on the elegant outlines of mountains was that of an old fire on company gathered round, illumining the essence of things.

Have you ever watched something so beautiful for so long that for just a minute you became a part of it? I watched until I was a part of that light, part of the land. A part of creation and creator. What shocked me was not my dissolution but the relief it brought. It was like a quiet rising of water. It was not erasure; it was inclusion, a connection so complete it mingled molecules. I was here, and I was part of the Arctic, and it was part of me.

The wind died, and the night air lay balmy on my skin. And then south down the wide river valley a rainbow appeared against the mountain to the east, curving out over the valley. It brightened, extended its arc, and then disappeared. Then another appeared farther down the valley. Then another, claiming the valley and all that was in it. And then a double rainbow!

The previous summer in Anchorage, during the week of the funeral, dark clouds built each afternoon, releasing furious torrents. Our priest told me after the funeral that he had seen eight rainbows that week. I had only noticed the storms.

I could not restrain myself from laughing out loud, just laughing in the Arctic night. Just as quickly I felt foolish, and I knew definitively that I was not alone.

Requiem
Tuba Mirum

The canticle [can be called] the "sword of the spirit," because it provides a weapon for those who virtuously fight against the invisible spirits; for the word of God, taking possession of the spirit when sung or spoken, has power to drive away demons.

— *Quaestiones et responsiones ad Orthodoxos* 107 (**PG 6.1354**)

I hear the voices around me. I am swallowed up in them. I close my eyes and sink into the sound slowly, like a sigh.

Every Monday night beginning in September, two months after the funeral, I come to the rehearsal hall, sit in the hard folding chair. I bring water in a heavy red plastic bottle Dad and Kathy had with them on the river. It is scratched from use and still has sand around its rim from the river. I refuse to wash it. The first rehearsal, I sit next to Deb, who is only a few years older than me, with stylishly graying hair in long, thick curls. We had both gone to business school, both loved to sing. She doesn't have a car, so I drive her home after rehearsals. We become fast choir friends.

The ancient idea of *koinonia*, unity in diversity. *Propter chorum*, say the monks. For the sake of the choir. Surely each of us here has a grief for which they sing, whether or not they know it. I need this unity, a connection to others, something that tells me I am present. But I am singing selfishly, for myself, hoping for a way out of this pain.

I want there to be a reason that I am here, a sign that proves this is good and right.

The night of my audition, the rain had just stopped when I arrived home to my apartment in a quiet neighborhood in the city. I walked up the dark sidewalk, a path bordered by a towering spruce tree and thick rhododendrons. The faint light filtering from neighboring windows lit the slick surface of the flagstones, shiny from the September rain, just enough to see my way to the door. As I made my way up the gentle curve of stairs, my mind back at the audition, a sudden *whoosh* startled me out of my skin. The *whoosh* came again and I jumped back just in front of the outstretched wings of an enormous owl. The friction of feathers snatched the air, decelerating his body, and the owl landed, suddenly silent, on the electrical pole just on the edge of the sidewalk. My heart raced and my skin felt cool. I had never seen an owl anywhere in the city, and certainly nowhere close to my apartment. I stood transfixed, saturated in the silence, the silhouette, the sound of the pounding of my heart in my neck. When I finally turned to walk to my door, his stare was as palpable as the movement of air beneath his wings.

A week later, an emailed acceptance appeared in my in-box. Relief and exhilaration rushed into my muddled brain, cooling water over coals of grief. I would be able to sing Mozart's Requiem. I had something I could do for Dad and Kathy. This was my Kaddish; this was the structure for my grief.

⋏

Deb is the first person to whom I confess the events of the summer and the reason for my joining the chorale. I am surprised at her lack of surprise. We are a month into rehearsals, and as the director works with the men on a section, I whisper to her, a flood of information draining from me in desperation.

"This bottle is from their trip." She nods at me. "And this sand? It's still here from the river, from the beach where they died. I haven't washed it off. Think that makes me crazy?" I laugh nervously, appalled that I have admitted my neurosis, exposed weakness and oddity and an indication that I am seriously screwed.

She shrugs. "Not really," she says.

I take a drink. The fine sand crunches lightly between my teeth.

The conductor looks back in our direction. "Okay, altos, sopranos — join us, top of forty, measure three."

I flee my anxiety, diving deeper into the black notes on the white page, the sounds of sorrow and hope and pleading, submersing myself in the music, feeling it close over me like water.

CHAPTER 7

A PRECARIOUS LIFE

No one ever told me that grief felt so like fear.

–C. S. Lewis, *A Grief Observed*

[Man] can do nothing by natural instinct except weep!... To man alone in the animal kingdom is granted the capacity for sorrow ... to no animal is assigned a more precarious life.

–Pliny, *Natural History*

A picture shows my father in front of a U.S. Forest Service log cabin in the woods of Alaska, tall, lean, handsome, with thick black hair and an optimistic grin untainted by tragedy or other devastation, the stance of a young and virile man who has stepped firmly into his place in the world of accomplishment and adventure well beyond his origins. He holds me, an infant just five months old. The photo is dated August 1972. It is thirteen years after Alaska became the forty-ninth state, a year before the oil crisis of 1973 prompted construction of the Trans-Alaska Pipeline. I am the first child and daughter of an army JAG captain and his wife sent at the last minute to Alaska instead of Vietnam. We were just one family among many compelled to move to Alaska because of oil industry employ or military service, and one of the many who, once acquainted with Alaska's remote beauty, decided to stay.

I was actually the second child; an older brother was stillborn at seven months and buried in the Fort Richardson cemetery. Perhaps that is why I was baptized within a week of birth in the post chapel, wearing a gown, booties, and cap my mother crocheted of fine ivory yarn and run through with pink ribbon. I was not a docile child; one story goes that I screamed so loudly in the hospital nursery that I was always fed first. My baby book notes that I logged more than one hundred miles of backpacking around Alaska in my first year, including a crossing of the Resurrection Trail. When I was nine months old, my parents and close friends bundled me up and strapped me to their backs and cross-country skied among the deep tracks of moose and the marks of scurrying porcupine into another Forest Service cabin for my first Christmas. The story goes that I woke up screaming in the subzero temperatures in the dark of night because I was too hot, and my father bumped his head on the upper bunk jumping up to tend to me.

I was born on the Ring of Fire. Anchorage, Alaska, sits in the middle of the long, horseshoe-shaped series of oceanic trenches, volcanic arcs, volcanic belts, and plate movements circling the Pacific. There were nights I woke to the lurching and shuddering of the earth, the sudden subterranean slide of the coastline away from the steadily moving Pacific Plate. Dad would round us up to stand beneath the downstairs doorways until the quake passed. Eight years before I was born, the Good Friday earthquake of 1964 crippled the state. The Pacific Plate shifted suddenly under the Northwest Plate, the earth buckled and cracked, and houses and buildings were ripped in two, some falling into the sea. Buildings shook as far away as Seattle, and the earth in Houston temporarily surged four inches. Geologists say that for weeks, long period-waves traveled the earth, with seiches — sloshing water as in a bathtub, but on an oceanic scale — reported as far away as South Africa, and that aftershocks from this quake continued for a year. After I was born, other than the odd object falling off a shelf, earthquakes never caused harm.

But perhaps I should have seen the signs. I was born on the Ring of Fire. I had always thought of myself as born in Alaska. This distinction makes a difference.

I started life with two parts of me in conflict: the part that drew rainbows and unicorns, and the part that wanted the carpentry sets Max and Ned received when Sam was born instead of the tea set I was given. We moved from the military base to a midcentury split-level house in the foothills of the Chugach Mountains when I was only a year old. The walls were decorated with Alaskan art, and a large gold velvet sofa sat in the living room. Our meals were made of the more limited provisions available in Alaska: frozen vegetables and powdered milk and Tang and otherwise heavy but not epicurean Midwestern-inspired fare. I remember one egg casserole made with Spam. My mom decorated my room in orange and green. As a toddler and a young child, I could sit for hours drawing on paper without other entertainment, something that must have proved handy for my parents. I started music lessons when I was three and studied piano for a decade. My mom taught my brothers and me to read chapter books before we were five, and read us Greek myths and history for fun between hauling us to piano lessons and soccer games. We were allowed little TV, if any, as children, only occasionally watching *Mister Rogers* or *The Electric Company* on a tiny black-and-white television in the kitchen. Later we watched *Mutual of Omaha's Wild Kingdom* as a family once a week. I remember an occasional episode of *Gilligan's Island* well after it was syndicated, and sneaking out to watch over the balcony when my parents bought a small color TV to watch the miniseries *Shogun* and *The Winds of War.*

I started swimming at six, running at eight, and skiing as a teenager. The summer I was ten, my mom dropped off my brothers and me for lunchtime runs with Dad from his midtown office, and we ran 10k races on the weekends. At one point Sam had the third fastest time in the nation for a five-year-old running a 10K.

He may have been one of three five-year-olds who ever ran a 10K. I continued swimming competitively most of the way through high school. In many ways, our life in Anchorage was not unique from those who lived in any other American city of similar size, other than an appreciation for and acceptance of the wildness around us remembered by the regular visits of moose, the practice of earthquake drills in elementary school, and an awareness of Cold War fears that manifested in my drawing designs for houses with complex bomb shelters.

When I was ten, we moved to the house I remember as my home, farther up the hillside, surrounded by more than an acre of forest. It was modern for its time in the early 1980s. We moved at the height of the economic boom, which collapsed only a few years later, at the same time my parents' marriage fell apart. I anchored myself in that home in the midst of our family's disintegration. It sat in the foothills of the Chugach, which formed a fortress, a high protectorate. The mountains stood as sentinels, points of reference no matter where I might be. I had the smallest room, but one with windows on one side and a balcony with a sliding glass door on the other, looking out to the mountains behind, the city below and the sea beyond. Orion, the hunter, marched across the sky at night, club and shield in hand, belt glistening, from the shale arêtes of the Chugach, above the spruce and birch forests, and around our house to the rainbow strip of reflection that was Cook Inlet, across which Mount Susitna, the Sleeping Lady, reclined. Ursa Major and Ursa Minor traversed the sky too, Big Bear and Little Bear. I had read the myths: Zeus turning the beautiful goddess Callisto and her son into bears and flinging them into the sky to protect them from his jealous wife, Hera. Part of Ursa Major made up our Alaska state flag, the Big Dipper, "eight stars of gold on a field of blue," as the state song goes. Polaris, the North Star, is one of those eight stars. This world around me, mountains, stars, and sea, told me I was safe. As did waking in that room to find my door nudged-open in the night by my dad roaming the house to check on everyone while we slept.

Dad introduced us to the Chugach Mountains as we grew. One year we ascended Flattop as the weather came in; Dad carried Sam, still a small boy, on his shoulders on the way down as we tried to beat the storm, losing his hat to the wind. I cried unreasonably. I'd liked Dad's hat, and it was gone, and we raced the rain to the car and I felt the urgency of danger. Another year we kids scrambled up the rocky O'Malley Peak with Dad, reaching the ridge and then false peak after false peak, finally signing our names on the ledger in the hard plastic tube at the top. I knew the contours of the mountains and valleys on each side of Flattop Mountain, and had camped in the mountains beyond what was visible from the city in each direction.

My mom divorced my dad when I was twelve, explaining that she just didn't love him anymore. This act shattered an idyllic childhood into shards that continued to slice our souls and each other decades later, and introduced doubts like many-headed monsters into my pubescent and faltering sense of self-worth. She reveled in her newfound freedom. Dad bent under the weight of betrayal and financial hardship.

The things I remember:

Eating out at Denny's frequently, and Dad jumping up from his Asian stir-fry with the other men in the restaurant when a domestic dispute turned physical in the parking lot; unlike the other men, who clustered inside the door, Dad continued through and pulled the man away from the woman to allow her to escape.

Eating at a little Italian restaurant called One Guy from Italy in a strip mall off Northern Lights that looked just like every other strip mall sprouting across the oil-money-infused and minimally zoned city of Anchorage. Dad inevitably got tomato sauce on his tie.

Dad trying to make lasagna for us one night, and becoming irate when I told him he needed to boil the noodles first. That's when I started to help cook.

Dad trying to do our laundry, and shrinking my favorite striped Esprit outfit, which wasn't supposed to be put in the dryer. That's when I started doing my own laundry.

Having to put Tampax on the shopping list for Dad in silent mortification, which became exponentially worse when he brought home the wrong kind.

I remember the insidious financial strain as Dad navigated a divorce and ran a small law practice that, like the rest of the Alaskan economy, was utterly dependent on oil revenues and staggered under the oil crash of 1986 and the crippling state recession that followed. I remember Dad showing up to our swim practices exhausted from work and sitting in the bleachers, his shoulders sagging with fatigue. I remember asking Dad why he was doing so much with the swim team board and at church when he was so tired and working so hard. "'To whom much is given, much is expected,'" he quoted with a tiredness that ran deeper than I could comprehend. I always knew him, throughout his life, to volunteer in meaningful and behind-the-scenes ways, and he did so with joy, his manner and execution learned from his parents before him. I remember putting together a party for Dad, trying to imitate what we had seen grown-ups do in earlier years, wanting somehow to acknowledge his Herculean efforts. I hung a sign in the kitchen that said "We love you Dad!" and cut up carrots on a platter served next to a bowl of ranch dressing.

I learned quickly, as kids do, how to adapt, constructing a facade of success that I wielded like a shield. In high school I was president of the debate team, captain of the swim team, and editor of the literary magazine, which we laid out with paper and glue. I figured out what I needed to do to get mostly A's in honors classes at my large public high school, and didn't do more. I learned that if I kept busy by doing a lot of things and doing them well, I didn't have to think about anything I wanted to avoid; I could get the attention a first child craves, and be excused from things I wanted nothing to do with, like family counseling. If I performed, I was left alone. As soon as I had my driver's license at sixteen, I moved my small stash of things from my mom's house, where we spent every other week, back up to Dad's house on a day when he was in Kodiak for business.

Five years after the divorce, Dad met and married Kathy, an elementary school teacher only a couple of years younger than he was with a quick smile and an easy laugh, light-blue eyes, and rosy cheeks. They married the summer I left for college. I regarded my new stepmom with considerable wariness. I went along when she scheduled a color assessment for me, coaxing me beyond my tomboyish ways. I wore the clothes she bought. She treated me as a daughter at times and a friend at others. I welcomed and resisted both. Though craving maternal affection, I didn't want to recognize the shift in dynamics in our household. We weren't any of us so different from the bull moose that wandered across our lawn. We sparred to establish dominance — my father as parent, me as teenager growing into an adult; my stepmother defining her new role, me resisting change to the precarious settlement of earlier family brokenness. We left a few antler prongs on the ground. Once focused exclusively on us kids, Dad found happiness with his new wife. I was too self-absorbed to worry about parental satisfaction. My one aim in life had been to please my father. I didn't know what to do if he was no longer as interested. The dynamic of women in a household could chafe through civility at times to reveal a hardness as sharp as the shale on the Chugach behind our home.

Despite the challenges, Kathy brought a beauty and an elegance to our lives that I loved, even as she managed our home with a fastidiousness beyond my tolerance. She and Dad remodeled the entire house soon after they were married, making it their own, and rules changed to maintain its shiny newness. I grumbled during each visit home from college. Kathy was focused on managing her house. I just wanted to relax at home. I was the less gracious of the two of us.

Dad and Kathy now volunteered together, serving as a Big Couple to a young boy in downtown Anchorage; they worked in the church, doing everything from serving on the vestry to washing windows and delivering food from the church's food kitchen.

Reluctantly, I learned from Kathy to appreciate beautiful things, to set a lovely table, to put together healthy and inspired meals. She shared my ideas too, adopting the latte I liked as her new coffee drink, and asking me about recipes I was trying. We made pie crusts together and my favorite lingonberry-orange-nut bread.

We also began spending time at the log cabin just south of Denali that Kathy brought to the marriage. The cabin became a place of making new family memories untainted by brokenness. On Dad and Kathy's final Thanksgiving, Peter and I drove to the cabin with Dad. Peter was the only romantic interest I'd ever brought home. Kathy had arrived a day early, and in the rudimentary kitchen prepared a feast: turkey and stuffing, sweet potatoes and brown sugar, beans, four different kinds of homemade pies. Having heard that Peter liked Honest Tea (we usually enjoyed hot tea in the evenings), Kathy bought a case of it at Costco. Dad and Kathy shared photos and stories from their Canning River trip the year before; Kathy taught us all yoga poses she knew as she studied to become an instructor in her teaching retirement; all of us enjoyed a day in the snow, Peter and me on snowshoes and Dad and Kathy on mountain bikes with studded tires. As we headed out that day, Peter snapped a picture of Dad and Kathy that captured such joy as they laughed under their balaclavas, hats, and helmets that we later used it as one of two primary images for their funeral and to distribute to friends. Looking at the photo later, again and again, I saw the creases in Dad's face mapping both greater sorrow and greater joy, both more pain and more understanding, than did the photo of him in front of that Forest Service cabin when I was a baby.

After I left for college and then the army, before every Christmas and Thanksgiving, a heavy, shoebox-sized package arrived wherever I was living at the time. Inside was a gift from Kathy, on behalf of both her and Dad (but Dad didn't bake): a tinfoil-wrapped loaf of lingonberry-orange-nut bread. The loaf embodied the sweet tartness of cold fall days and recalled memories of picking berries a few months before on my Labor Day visits. The gift expressed love when words didn't come easily; the sweetness of the bread balancing the acerbic taste of lingonberries was a promise to work through the challenge of reconstructing a family.

As they approached retirement, Dad and Kathy explored more and more of the rivers of Alaska, choosing a sport that did not tax Dad's failing knees. They fell in love with the Arctic. I once prompted Dad to consider taking a vacation somewhere more exotic, Italy maybe, where he might enjoy opera and red wine, and he laughed and said he would never see all he wanted to of Alaska and didn't really see any point in going anywhere else. After working hard for decades at his law practice, Dad glimpsed the life he imagined and knew his time was limited. He and Kathy were living it.

Λ

And in the middle of living it, they died, leaving their bodies on a distant riverbank. In the middle of my living, I received the fateful call in Portland while visiting Sam. How can we ever appreciate the full depth of each moment? Is there any way not to look back on those last conversations, last meetings, wishing we had let them seep into us completely?

Hanging up after my brief conversation with Officer Holschen, a few words in a matter of minutes altering my life forever, I sat in time suspended. Then motion resumed, making up for the pause, and never seeming to stop, though always just outside of a fog surrounding me. Leaving Portland, I started a checklist as Sam drove.

I was the oldest. I felt responsible for doing whatever needed to be done—and, most important, for making sure it was done right. Why I thought I had the ability to do this, I'm not sure. Perhaps it was the hubris of the eldest child. Perhaps it was what Joan Didion has called the "shallowness of sanity."

A muddy sense of the necessary—though how could I know what was necessary?—drove my actions and phone calls. I called Max and Ned and left messages; Ned and his wife were traveling, we thought, back from a trip to Indonesia. We looked for alternate numbers to reach them, calling friends and work, and left messages everywhere we could, with only the request to call back as soon as possible. I knew I could not call Grandma or Kathy's mother directly, as both were elderly and I thought it would be better to have someone tell them in person, so I called aunts and uncles to find someone to deliver the news. I called Peter. Despite our recent breakup, my connection to him was my closest and most necessary, in part because of his relationship with Dad and Kathy. He said that he would meet us in Seattle on our way to the airport, then come to Alaska a few days later.

Then we called our mom, who lived with her husband in Anchorage and who answered like anyone would on a normal Sunday. Call after call, and again and again the people on the other end of the line went into variations of incredulous hysterics. It was absurd; horror shares an edge with hilarity. Each conversation started like a sick joke. I almost snickered a couple of times, a weird and subconscious acknowledgment of the disbelief on the other end of the line, understanding how ludicrous the call must sound to unexpecting ears, wanting to let down my own defenses but afraid I would never recover.

I didn't have time or energy to help those I spoke with to maneuver through their responses. And shouldn't I be the one in hysterics? I wanted to beg for people to be gentle, to be calm, because there was only the thinnest thread holding me together, and if they were too distraught, I might collapse. I cut conversations short with a sense of guilt and inadequacy. In an instant, all of my emotional reserves had evaporated, the way a fiery explosion consumes a tree, all at once. I had nothing left, feeling only a numbness and a shock I understood much later to be a blessing, a natural anesthetic for the crippling pain.

At SEA-TAC airport, I watched Sam, to see if I could help him somehow. He stared blankly out the terminal window. Sitting next to his wife, I looked without seeing at the *People* magazine she had brought me. "Mind candy," she said. But she overestimated my capabilities. I couldn't even open the cover. The magazine sat on my lap, a dead and useless thing. Despite the flurry of planning in those first five hours, my brain was foggy, and I had the feeling of stumbling along a craggy Chugach mountainside, lost in clouds that had engulfed the mountain.

We arrived in Anchorage June 26. At that time of year, even at 10:30 p.m., bright daylight reflected off the snow in the Chugach. The sun's persistence — the same sun which had illuminated extended hours of running through the yard when I was a child — now felt like an interrogation. Exhausted, I squinted into it through the airplane windows as the plane taxied to the terminal.

Walking off the plane, I held my breath as though preparing for a gut blow. I would have welcomed it in lieu of the gaping, jagged hole of Dad's absence. I looked around blankly, expecting everyone to understand the horror I felt, the appalling emptiness. Instead I saw a scattering of unfamiliar faces, not looking at me or understanding, searching for other faces, smiling. It was odd that each of these people could not see the rupture of the world, that they could not understand that bedrock had cracked.

On every previous trip home, at least twice a year for fifteen years, Dad towered over the other greeters, usually just to the left rear of the crowd. His eyes embraced me well before his arms could, his enthusiasm and excitement to have his kids come home the focus of his attention. Kathy was always standing next to him, tall, lean, and smiling. After college, years in the army, graduate school, and finally settling in Seattle, I made that trip home twice a year. Dad's and Kathy's jackets changed from heavy down in winter to windbreakers in summer, and Dad's hair changed from jet black to sprinkled with salt, alarmingly more so lately, I thought. But his eyes never dimmed.

As my mind travels back through each moment of that dark night, the fear of revisiting the pain in those times and places is matched only by what I have ceased to think of as an ironic fear of losing that pain and those memories.

A year before Dad and Kathy died, I'd been on a mission trip to El Salvador with my church. Our last two days in country we spent on the beach. I swam in the ocean, out beyond a strong surf. Another man on our team called to me, and I swam over to him. His eyes were wide. Seeing his terror, I took his arm. I yelled at him to swim with his other arm, but his fear paralyzed him. I held on to him, sidestroking as strongly as I could, focusing on the beach, and trying not to notice the rolling and pounding froth in front of us, the force of the water pulling my body. The surf pulled us toward the rocks. Despite a sinking sense of failure, I continued a strong stroke, my strongest stroke. At last, we broke through the surf, just before the sea would have thrown us on the rocks. I pulled him into shallow water, walked him onto shore.

This was different. Now it was my eyes that were wide. Waters overwhelmed me; there was no shore in sight. There was no one to call. I struggled in vain, sinking deeper, vaguely aware of a cold pressure building, flashes of light far above, but feeling the uselessness of struggle as I descended into darkness. I could not take a stroke. The froth overcame me. I could barely breathe. I did not know to cry out. I had no words for prayer.

The first night in Anchorage, I slept on the couch in my mother's house. I had never stayed in her house when visiting Anchorage, considering my home to be with my dad. She had picked us up from the airport, giving us hugs and having as few words as we did. We arrived late. We could go to the house I knew as home in the morning. I lay awake, staring at the ceiling, unable to sleep because of the light and the horrible chiming of a grandfather clock. My mind traveled at the speed of my flight home — faster, even — without navigation or destination, pinging through space.

At 2:00 a.m. the phone rang. I answered. It was Ned.

Ned was adopted when we were all too young to remember. We were not close; in fact, our proximity in age made us rivals. Our youthful interaction involved his angry lashing out and my cynical disdain. As he grew older, Dad had kept Ned's expressions of anger in check with a firm hand. In recent years, Ned seemed to have grown into a bright and capable man, marrying a woman toward whom he seemed tender, earning advanced degrees in market research and landing a prestigious job at a large company in Philadelphia. At the rare gathering since then, his physical threats had mostly subsided, and our verbal sparring dissipated with the years. We hadn't had any experiences to build a bond in the wake of our clashes, though, so I cared for him cautiously.

Someone had already told him what had happened. Through a hazy consciousness, I heard his voice, scratchy through the phone, stammering, alternating between hoarse and screechy.

"I know," I said again and again, because I didn't know what else to say. "Don't worry about anything here. We'll take care of it. Just get here when you can. The funeral's not till Thursday." Hanging up, I laid back down and went back to staring at the ceiling in the relentless midnight light.

In the days to come, I focused on a discrete set of activities. Church, funeral home, music, notifications, obituary, burial, house. I waded through the narrow muffled tunnel of what was required and what I thought I could control. And yet when the organist, a longtime friend of Dad and Kathy's and an accomplished musician, offered to help with the music, I was relieved and grateful. Looking back, it's clear that while I thought I was handling a host of details, everything came together because of an outpouring of support, usually silent, from people at church, friends of Dad's and Kathy's, parents of friends of mine from growing up.

I had always thought that when Dad died I would collapse in a heap. I had even envisioned it: years from now getting a call at my office, letting out a cry and a wail, having to be carried out because my legs would not support me. It was one of the things I was most terrified of. And yet halfway through the week, I had not cried at all.

Peter flew in on Tuesday. I waited at the airport, which might have been another planet. I was a void, a hole where a person used to be, a black cutout of space. People came through the security gate meeting friends and families with smiles and hugs. I stared at them. They looked two-dimensional, figures from magazines.

Though I was surrounded by strangers at the airport, I was glad to be away from the house and the planning. I sat on the plastic terminal chairs, staring at Dad's and Kathy's pictures on the cover of the *Anchorage Daily News.* We had decided not to talk to the press. The newspaper printed a picture of Kathy in long braids and a windbreaker taken twenty-five years prior next to Dad's serious but handsome picture from the website of the law firm he had founded three decades earlier. The headline was large and bold: "Victims of Improbable Attack Were Wilderness Vets." The connection to me, to Dad and Kathy, seemed unlikely, impossible. I stared as though trying to interpret a foreign language.

For many months after, it took every ounce of emotional energy I had to get through a given day. I had no buffer. Remembering to eat was a problem. That first week, Dad's sister, Aunt Marcia, reminded me, "Have a little something, just a bite of protein." I ate one bite of whatever was at hand. It tasted like nothing. Peter fielded phone calls. The idea of talking to anyone, even well-wishers, even friends, was exhausting. Peter proofread and formatted the funeral bulletin. He slept on a trundle bed next to mine, holding my hand.

The boys' wives headed out to pick up the tan-colored heavy paper I wanted to hold the funeral bulletin, and the green ribbon I wanted to tie it together. The church told us they were expecting six hundred or more people. Aunts and uncles helped fold and tie the programs together, but hadn't expected to do so many.

"Do you want to just put ribbons on the programs for family?" asked my mom, who was helping to coordinate. "There are a lot of them; this will take time."

"No, let's tie ribbons on all of them," I said.

"Shannon, you have to understand what this is about," said Sam's wife, smiling.

I looked at her quickly, and spoke slowly, my eyes weighted with lead, my words made of acid. "Don't tell me what this is about," I said. "I know exactly what this is about." I am not proud of my unkindness. My focus was reptilian: looking purely on doing what I thought needed to be done, and doing it as well as possible. She cringed, wilting, and I don't know that we ever fully recovered.

Ned arrived later than expected. My uncle Tom picked him up from the airport. "The flight was cancelled," Ned said. "They were trying to reschedule all of us, and there was a long line of people trying to go on their stupid cruises and fishing trips. I just yelled, 'My dad was killed by a flipping bear, and you're worried about your fishing trips?'" He laughed. "They moved me to the front of the line."

I looked at him with disgust and walked into another room. He was proud of how he had acted? He thought that honored Dad and Kathy? He thought it was okay to act that way? I didn't know how it could be that this man and I shared the same family. His reaction polluted a sacred if confusing time. I tried to put it aside.

Later that day Uncle Tom came into the dining room, where we were making final edits to the service bulletin. "I don't know what you're all thinking," he said, "but I'd take the living room set if no one else wants it."

I stared at him, trying not to scream and not to cry, and looked back at the computer.

"We haven't talked about it yet," said Sam.

The week of the funeral, thunder announced the approach of black clouds rolling over the Chugach Mountains. I did not remember ever having heard thunder in Alaska. I did not remember there ever having been such dark clouds. I knew that there was another power here, unseen, even unfelt. I was doing what humans do in these times, looking for signs, for symbols, for something to lend meaning, but felt flattened, stretched, and dried, an animal skin put out to cure, cracking from exposure. Sun broke through the clouds, sometimes tentatively, sometimes suddenly. Then it poured rain, as briefly as a passing sound. And then there were the rainbows I'd hear about later. It was too hard for me then to see past the storms.

Dad's older sister, my aunt Georgia, stayed in Arizona to care for Grandma, who wasn't able to travel. On the phone, Aunt Georgia recalled a conversation during Dad and Kathy's April visit in which they had talked about end-of-life planning. She remembered that Dad and Kathy mentioned wanting to be buried in Healy, a small town four hours' drive north of Anchorage and close to our family cabin. But Anchorage is where all of us, including Kathy, had spent our lives. Anchorage is where Dad and Kathy lived even as they planned for more and more time in the wild and at the cabin after Kathy retired from teaching and Dad neared retirement from law. Most of the people we knew, or who knew them, lived close to Anchorage. I called Dad and Kathy's friend Shorty to ask about the cemetery in Healy. He said that he would take care of it. And I coordinated with our home church of St. Mary's for the funeral.

Our community at St. Mary's Episcopal Church was more of a constant in my life than our family structure or the house we lived in. We went to church as a family at the A-frame building in midtown Anchorage from as early as I can remember, and we kids were confirmed there. Dad and Kathy were married there. Dad had been raised Baptist, my mom Lutheran, and they started coming back to church when I was born. "I was willing to barter with my own soul, but not the souls of my children," Dad wrote in a journal. He told me of the spiritual legacy he believed the women in his family had passed down, a joyful and strong faith. He spoke of this faith as the greatest of all treasures.

St. Mary's had experience with Alaska's brutalities too. Ten years earlier, another parishioner, Marci Trent, and her son and grandson were on a trail run when they came across a brown bear defending a moose carcass. Marci and her son were killed. Her fourteen-year-old grandson climbed a tree when he heard the commotion and was rescued. Marci was seventy-seven years old, well known and loved among the many communities of which she was a part, including the long-distance running community, in which she held several age-group world records. We saw her not only at church but in the 10K races we entered with Dad. Her son was a well-known musician and music teacher. The *New York Times* told the story on July 3, 1995, ten years to the day before we buried Dad and Kathy. "Mrs. Trent had suffered massive injuries to her head and chest, while Mr. Waldron had apparently bled to death from a severed artery in his leg." A later account notes that her spine and neck had been broken. It had seemed bizarre, horrific, isolated. Not something that would happen to someone we knew. Certainly not something that would happen again. A freak accident.

Maybe it was because of this that I never asked why, never asked the question that has no answer.

Thursday afternoon, our priest observed the Episcopal ritual of receiving the coffins as they arrived at the church. At the front doors, he draped the coffins with vestments, red and white. He prayed. He walked ahead of the draped caskets as they were rolled in and placed side by side in front of the altar, placed where weeks before Dad and Kathy stood in line to take communion. The Episcopal funeral liturgy celebrates the resurrection of Christ. The priest had begun our formal ceremony of grief, and of celebration.

In the hour before the service, the only semblance of a wake we held, I stood at the coffins with a few others. I remember only Aunt Marcia. I remember a gutteral sound coming from her throat, and wanting to claim it, because I didn't have any sounds, and wanting her there, because I needed someone to love me and say it was okay, but also wanting her gone, because I wanted the space to myself. At first we each circled the coffins warily, or perhaps it was our grief we were aware of then, keeping a distance to keep us safe. I finally laid a hand on one of them with care, as though it might scald at the touch, and then let the weight of my arm sink down, and there was so much weight. Aunt Marcia put both hands on the coffins. And then she closed her eyes and tilted back her head and started to sing "Holy, Holy, Holy." For a moment I stood mortified, shocked by the nakedness of faith and grief exposed by the singing voice, exposed and magnified like holding up a glass to the sun. And then I joined her, my voice less sure, more childlike, our hands pressing down with the impossible weight of sadness on the hard surfaces of coffins lying quiet beneath the vestments.

I don't know whether I came back to the Episcopal Church at the time of the funeral, or if it came back to me. I'd left it in grad school, fed up with the church's involvement in politics. I'd attended a Presbyterian church instead. But brought to my knees in life, I came back. It was the liturgy I had missed, the liturgy containing in its words and seasons a wisdom surpassing its parts. I felt the familiar rhythm in the prayers and music I knew.

I believed that these connected to the sacred — believed it, but at the time did not feel it. And I did not feel that this rhythm and structure containing millennia of study and prayer quietly and invisibly built a foundation under me. I was grateful for the things to do, the things that must be done, even without understanding their importance. I felt nothing other than the vague sense that I must somehow survive this funeral, survive this day, survive the rest of my life.

At the funeral, melodies from Handel's *Messiah* lilted through the congregation, seemed to swirl around me, hold me, encircle the coffins, and soar to the mountains just outside the windows that formed the front wall of St. Mary's. I spoke, and Kathy's brother spoke. I'd cobbled together words only that morning at Peter's urging. I knew our faith celebrates resurrection, and so I tried to be upbeat, and it all fell flat, because resurrection does not come without crucifixion, and you cannot celebrate Easter without living Good Friday.

Through that wall of windows behind the altar, the clouds lifted around sharp ridgelines still crusted with snow and the deep valleys of the Chugach. These were the mountains that framed my city, that had framed my life with Dad as I grew. Memories played out shallowly, etchings on a glass: running with dogs, a tent blowing down in the middle of the night, dog paws cut by scree. And then the memories disappeared, and I stared at the mountains because they were familiar, and because they were there.

The thing about these times is that you are constantly battered by stupidity and selfishness when you are least equipped to handle it. After the service, as we walked out of the front doors of the church, someone asked if they could take a photo of us. I looked at the woman with exhausted and unbelieving eyes. "This is my father's funeral. There will be no pictures today," I said. Later that week my uncle Tom said, "Well, there must be some money for you kids, right?" None of us responded. Furniture and photos and money.

The thing about these times is that you are given more kindnesses than you can ever know. Before the service, I saw a man from the congregation setting up a video camera so we could send a copy of the service to Grandma; he had taken the day off work to find a way to put everything together. After the service, the choir director came up with a gentle smile and offered tapes of the Bach Magnificat in which Dad had sung a solo. One of the other men in the choir came up with watery eyes and handed me a rose the choir had placed on Dad's chair. I've tried to recall these things, to go back and see them and hold them in memory, and know I will never begin to know them all. And I also know that these kindnesses far outnumber the insensitivities.

Our priest at the church told me that Kathy had been visiting an old student of hers every week in prison, and that now he would start making those visits for her.

One of the Laotian refugees who had lived with us for six months when I was ten years old came up to me: "Shannon, be strong," he said.

An Inupiat man with kind eyes and dressed in a dark suit had traveled from Barrow. He and Dad had worked together for decades. He wanted to say hello, and that he was sorry.

We smiled and talked to people we had not seen in years. The reception felt oddly like some sort of respectable gathering highlighting social graces. I suppose in some ways it was. It felt vaguely — to the extent that I had any specific feelings — important to be strong, to represent Dad well. The priest I had grown up with, now retired, was there. I was taken aback by, though later thankful for, his words: "You kids don't know what's happening yet. In another four, maybe six weeks it will start getting really hard. Take care of yourselves."

The pews were packed with colleagues from the office and their families, people I knew from church, and many people I didn't know at all. This is when I started to understand something that would take me years to process: that each of us lives a thousand lives. "Each man is a universe," says Antoine de Saint-Exupéry. My selfish claims to grief were false; none of us who grieve have a corner on the market. Even if Dad was the most important person in my life, and Kathy right up there, I knew only pieces of them. They were part of a web of humanity, and the web was torn, and those of us who are left all have to do the work of repair. Grief is something we claim with even a passing knowledge of someone, rocked by the finality of death in the intimacy of its implications. They are in our lives, and then they aren't.

A few days later, one of Dad's colleagues shook his head and looked into the distance. "It's hard to believe," he said. "I saw him every day of the work week and some weekends for twenty-five years. I can't believe he's gone." I felt a twinge of jealousy. He'd spent more time with my dad than I had.

Burial was scheduled for the next afternoon, since Healy was a four-hour drive to the north. It rained on and off for the duration of the drive.

The cemetery in Healy sits on a hill framed by mountains of the Alaska Range. Dad and Kathy's friend Shorty, who lived nearby, said that he walked his dogs there every day. It was the place with the best view of the northern lights when they danced in fall and winter night skies. The tundra was decorated with early fireweed and lupine, a fence of spruce trees. Shorty had dug a perfectly square grave facing east to hold both coffins and hauled away most of the fill. Holy Mary of Guadalupe, the church Dad and Kathy attended when they were at the cabin, put together an interment service with music we had selected, played on guitar. Dad's army friend George and his wife, Joanne, stood off to the side next to a lone pine tree, as though unable to step any closer to that hole, as though standing next to the tree might protect them somehow.

Father Jack performed the service for our small group standing on the Alaskan tundra. The mountains stood witness, watching familiar scenes of death and grief that played like shadows on their slopes each day.

I stood at the corner of the chasm closest to Dad's coffin. My breath came shallowly, a susurrus leaking oxygen to reluctant blood. I knelt. I kissed the hard, cold surface of the coffin. The week caught up with me like a rifle shot. I touched the coffins with faltering fingers. Again. And again. The dark, gaping hole. The cold boxes. My legs gave way. I felt Peter's arms supporting me under my ribs. My abdominal muscles heaved against him, shuddering, fatigued. "Amazing Grace" played very far off in the distance. My awareness of needing to be in control, of needing to take care of things, collapsed. Things were taken care of. Now I did not know what could hold me together. In that music of life not constrained by time, a cacophony of sound overwhelmed the harmony I thought I knew.

There is no machinery to assist in a rural cemetery, where friends dig friends' graves. Several men helped lower each casket into the ground with thick straps. The weight was significant. The effort was clumsy. One of the boxes dipped. "Watch it!" Ned snarled, snatching the strap from one of the men lowering the heavy load. His lower jaw jutted out as he took over at the foot of the coffin. Briefly, through unfocused eyes, I noted his old anger emerging even in grief. I stayed pressed into Peter's body. Slowly these boxes, these sarcophagi, descended.

I suppressed the urge to reach out and hold onto them. I wanted to bring them back. I watched in horror as they were lowered unevenly, awkwardly, awfully, to final stillness, side by side in the Alaskan soil. What was in those boxes? Bodies, mangled human flesh and bone, no more. But it was physical evidence of the people I loved the most. I would never touch their cheeks again. They would never meet the husband I might have. Never know my children, their grandchildren. "I can't wait until the day we call to wish *you* a happy Mother's Day!" said Kathy when I called from

Korea on Mother's Day one year. It annoyed me then. Now I felt the loss of its possibility. I could not sit with them in their old age, telling and retelling stories, hearing final words of wisdom, walking next to them as their own deaths approached, learning from them how to die as they had taught me how to live. This never should have happened. It was an accident. It was done. It could not be undone. There was nothing to do.

Father Jack dipped a spruce bough in a bowl of water from the Nenana River and shook the bough toward the chasm in the earth. Three times, three sprays of the life of the river, the life of water: "In the name of the Father, and of the Son, and of the Holy Spirit." I didn't know what to do. I threw in a handful of dirt. It scattered with a light knock on the hard, hollow surface below.

A few people threw in sprigs of lupine picked from the tundra. The men picked up shovels. The first thuds of dirt. The echos. A spot of blue sky. Clouds. I felt kicked in the gut. I gagged. The strength of the shoveling belied things none of us could express. Singing voices mixed with wind and wide-open space. All strands of a rope that, even as I strangled against its fibers, formed the net binding us together, holding us up.

Most burials in the twenty-first century in the Western world are sterile. Astroturf covers the open grave. The casket sits quietly nearby while there is a short tribute. No one sees the casket descend, the machine-assisted descent. No one sees it covered up.

A rural funeral is different. It is raw, an open wound. It is like what is left of skin after sliding across asphalt at high speed. There was no way to make what was happening prettier. There was no way to make it less painful. And because it was exactly what it was meant to be, the intensity of the beauty, too, overwhelmed me, sharpening the blade of pain to an impossible severity. It cut me to the bone.

Peter and I drove back to the cemetery after light sustenance at the church. Shorty had finished filling in the grave. Flowers people had brought from Anchorage covered the even and neatly raked dirt and gravel. Peter held back. I walked over to sit next to the grave. A single sunflower. Its cheerfulness startled me. I thought that Grandma would like to know that Kansas, where Dad was born and reared, had been represented. I touched the flower. A firm stem, soft petals. Something solid, but it was a lie. What was here was not solid. What was here could not be explained. It was over. It had only begun.

That week was the beginning of a journey I still did not see the end of. I did not hear the river and the Arctic calling to me. The only thing I think I already knew was that this journey does not have an end.

CHAPTER 8

THE WEIGHT OF DAYS

Alas, what pointless and ignorant precision! We are counting the days when it is their weight we are seeking!

– Pliny, *Natural History*

At the end of our second day on the Hulahula, we swung the raft into a tiny eddy in a tertiary channel on the east side. From the river, an area of undulating tundra made up of wet tussocks spread the length of several football fields before the mountains rose steeply. We'd have plenty of warning if anything larger than a ground squirrel decided to visit our campground.

We found a moderately dry and flat place for our sleeping area. I walked the area looking for any animal sign, telltale grizzly scat or digging, but other than a couple of ground squirrel holes and caribou tracks, I didn't notice much. About fifty yards to the south, a broken dogsled sank into the tundra, its wood weathered and cracked. I looked with annoyance at a well-trod trail along the river; had humanity encroached so much on this faraway place it had to leave sign of its presence? Just as quickly, I was embarrassed. Noting the tracks left in the soft ground, I realized this was clearly a game trail, worn not by humans but by caribou, wolf, fox, bear. My city tendencies were quick to label and criticize, slow to listen and understand. I wasn't sure whether I'd come to this wild space to find myself or to lose myself, or whether I had the capacity for either.

My walk along the game trail reminded me of looking for tracks during my schoolgirl days, before I knew what I was hoping to find. Now I knew that my younger self was looking for clues to understand my world and myself in that world. It was a profitable search in the winter woods around our home in Alaska. The heavy narrow legs of moose dragged deep snow after them, their tracks disappearing onto a plowed road and turning up again on the other side. Sets of four footprints showed the movement of rabbits among the trees, the two large prints in back from their large hind feet. The wandering track of a wolverine on the side of a mountain. The light pencil-sketched tracks of birds scurrying for bits the trees dropped on the snow. In the mountains, the occasional imprint of a sheep's hoof and clustering of white wool where the group had stopped to rest. Tracks were adumbrations of the energy of life all about us, the recent history book of wilderness. I imagined the air quivering where the leaver of tracks had passed.

As we started to put up the tents, a guided group passed us and pulled in a hundred yards or so downriver. I watched them with a mix of frustration and relief. I wanted this to be my journey, not just one of several recreation trips. I wanted solitude, time and space to think, time and space to try to understand the memory held by this land that I didn't know but that was intimate to me. At the same time, the groups' proximity offered some comfort; statistically, bear attacks on groups larger than six are much more rare.

"I'll make dinner tonight," offered Sally.

"Can I help?" I asked.

"You can clean up," she said. "We'll all get our turns."

Sally fired up the hissing Coleman stove Ned had brought. It was strange to be here with two people I either didn't know or wasn't close to. Part of me wanted to debrief the day, what it had meant, and missed the trust required for that kind of conversation. I looked forward to my journal each night to make my own notes. Perhaps it was a reflection of grief; there is a long stretch of road that has to be traveled alone.

"I can't remember the last time I used anything more than a WhisperLite for camp meals," I said, searching for something to talk about in the present and recalling years of backpacking and mountain climbing trips. "A stove like this is luxury!"

"Welcome to the world of boaters," Sally smiled. "We don't have to worry about weight as much as you backpackers."

"Sure makes it easier to cook," I said. "Two burners too."

Suddenly we heard a yell. "The boat!" It was Ned.

The channel that had been running evenly several hours earlier now gushed with silty water, the current flowing deep and strong against and around the raft, almost separating it from camp. We pulled our dry suits up midstep, sprinting to the boat and the rushing water. Ned took the upstream side. I splashed in just below the boat and felt the heavy push of water at my waist, grabbed the chicken line to steady myself and jerked at it to move the raft back onto shore, but felt the boat turn with the water like a creature under its own power. The water shoved and yanked at my legs, shocking me with its force. I pulled against the line with all of my strength, pulled and prayed and screamed.

"Can you hold it?" I had to scream to be heard over the torrent.

"Trying!" Ned pulled at the boat with furrowed eyebrows and a scowl.

Sally had joined us, pulling on the landward side of the raft. "Try to walk it back onto the bank!" I yelled. She stepped backward toward the bank and pulled with great enthusiasm but little effect. Ned and I pushed with everything we had, steadying ourselves against the force of the river.

"Together!" I yelled. "Ready? One, two, three!" A shove and the raft inched onto the tundra.

"Again! One, two, three!" The raft lurched onto higher ground in a sudden release from the water. I heard the tundra vegetation scrape against the taut rubber. Staggering against the rushing water, I grabbed a willow branch to pull myself from the river. The three of us collapsed onto the tundra.

"Let's tie it off," I suggested, after we'd caught our breaths. "I don't think the river's going to get any higher, but you never know. Hard to raft without a boat."

"Good idea! Glad we got it!" chirped Sally.

"Nice job," I said, letting my voice carry the tension out of me and into the wind. I patted Sally on the back out of relief rather than congratulations

Ned grabbed the front line and tied it off to willows on two sides. It perched well above the new, higher water level with an annoying nonchalance.

But my pulse didn't stop pounding. How could we not have anticipated this danger? Of course the waters ran higher in the afternoon. The warmth of the day increases glacial melt upriver. We should have thought of this. Fear of the consequences of an error in such a remote place heightened my frustration. We had come here under the assumption, and with an unspoken agreement, that we would take care both of ourselves and of the places we traveled. If something went wrong here, it wasn't a question of sending someone down the road a mile to pick up an extra gallon of gasoline. People come to the wilderness with what they need, or they put others at risk or expense to compensate for their failures. We'd been lucky. Instead of disaster, we had another opportunity to know and understand this wilderness we were in. She had been gracious to us. We could not expect such grace to continue. I wondered again about the wisdom of our journey. But too late. We were committed.

We headed back to our kitchen area. Energy drained out of my body with each step.

"What are we having?" Ned asked.

"Cheese tortellini with spinach, pine nuts, and marinara. How's that sound?" asked Sally, pulling plastic bags out of one of the bear barrels.

"Incredible," I said, meaning it. "I've only had a Clif Bar all day."

"Water's ready for tea," Sally said, and poured from the kettle into the mugs we held out.

We sat around the stove, peeling off our dry suits and donning fleece. I dropped a teabag of Market Spice, my favorite Seattle tea loaded with cinnamon and orange, into my mug and closed my eyes, inhaling the aroma of comfort.

"Did you guys do much on rivers with your dad and Kathy?" Sally asked, checking the tortellini.

"Ned did," I said. "I went out on the Nenana with them once, but other than trips as a kid and sea kayaking in college, not much more." I regretted this. Dad and Kathy had talked about doing family trips, and Dad had written in his journal of wanting to take the family down the Colorado in the Grand Canyon, but I hadn't thought I needed any more hobbies.

"I did a few trips with them, and Dad and I would go out and play in the whitewater sometimes too," Ned said.

"What about you, Sally?" I asked.

"I got into it with my boyfriend just a couple of years ago," she said. "But we just do day trips."

"And you guys both go with the same group of people?"

"Yeah," Ned said. "We have, what . . ." he began.

"Maybe six or seven now," said Sally. "You guys want to hand me your bowls?"

She began serving the pasta, steam from the serving spoon curling into the cool air.

"Yeah," Ned said, "somewhere between five and ten people that get together on Saturdays to paddle."

"That's how you guys met?"

Sally nodded. "And then we found out we work in different parts of the same firm," she said. "Ned helped me carry my boat to the river the first day I came. He can be quite a gentleman."

"Really?" I smiled. "You hide these things well from some of the rest of us, Ned."

Ned smiled back.

"And even though you know Ned just from your kayaking group, you were willing to come along on a random trip in the middle of nowhere?" I asked Sally.

"I thought it would be fun!" Sally said.

"That's brave," I said. That's crazy, I thought. And brave.

"No one else was willing to go," said Ned.

"Gee, wonder why," I said. "Let's see, it's remote. And it's dangerous. And our reasons for choosing this stretch of river — well ..." I heard the doubt in my voice. Brave for Sally, foolish for me. Risking a river was one thing, but how was I going to handle arriving at Dad and Kathy's campsite? What did I think I could discover there?

After dinner I walked to the river to rinse our dishes. Crouching by the shore, I pulled up a handful of the rough tundra foliage to scour our bowls. Wild and wandering cries of birds accompanied the noise of the river, but I saw the birds at flight and from a distance. I wished I could identify them. Rainer Maria Rilke suggests that perhaps we are here only to name things. But I couldn't even accomplish that. I held one plastic dish in the river, letting the water fill it and spill over, again and again. I listened and watched for noticeable bird characteristics, something to identify them by. Several tiny birds flew with erratic modulations, and something that looked like a duck skimmed the surface of the river. All were too distant to see markings. Maybe it was better not to classify them, not to attempt to put them into a box, but simply to appreciate their presence out here in the gusty winds.

The water ran cold over my hands, and my fingers started to feel numb. I brought the dishes back to the kitchen. Sally and Ned were over at the sleeping tents.

The wind shifted and the temperature dropped. I added a layer of clothing and pulled on my wool hat, one that Peter's sister had given me two years ago for Christmas. Despite the chill, I was thankful for the fewer mosquitoes. The song and three-note trill of birds floated on the breeze, a melody of ABCA, and I recalled that ancient Jewish tradition says you can hear God in the songs of birds. If I could sit still enough to listen, maybe I could hear God too. Or at least take comfort in knowing that God was there, in that song, even if I didn't know how to understand. That part I believed.

After dinner, we walked down to say hello to the group downriver. Longtime Alaska guide Karen Jettmar and her assistant guide, Jamie, who was in his midtwenties, guided the group. Karen's pretty face, short hair, and cheerful but strict sense of order reminded me of Kathy. Dad and Kathy would have enjoyed talking with her. Ten clients clustered in a mosquito-netted eating tent. Jamie walked down to the bank of the river with us, and I compared my notes on flowers against his naturalist training.

I pulled out my journal and pointed out flowers on the tundra. "I have this as Eskimo potato," indicating a small sprig of purple flowers, "and this as mountain avens," indicating a small, white-petaled flower, "and this as woolly lousewort."

"Sure, mountain avens, shy maiden, Arctic lousewort, and elegant paintbrush for sure. That one is wild sweet pea, though, not Eskimo potato. They look similar, but you can see the difference in the leaves there."

"Right. I see. It's everywhere!" The focus on beauty salved my scorched soul. But could he tell? I grasped at meaning when I could find none. The flowers gave me something to look for, something to draw and make notes about, something to identify in a book with pictures.

"It is. Beautiful time of year for wildflowers."

"I can't believe how many there are! In some ways the limestone looks so plain, but then you come across these amazing flowers in the middle of it all."

"It's true, the Arctic is pretty special that way."

Kathy had identified the flowers on their river trips, and Dad had painted them on notecards when they returned. I loved Dad and Kathy more learning the same landscape they had loved, its wonders large and small. But despite, or perhaps because of, my determination, my connection to them felt shaky at best, and my attempts to find that connection awkward. It was the gossamer strand of the smallest spider's web, the final fragment of mist in a valley, a fragile dream of one-time meaning.

"How's your trip so far?" Jamie asked, his question intended for all three of us.

"Fine, fine," said Ned, not making eye contact.

"Just beautiful," I said. "We can't believe how warm it is!" Did I seem brave?

"I can't believe we're here without any beer!" Sally exclaimed cheerfully. "First time I've done something like *that!*"

"I'm tired enough, I'd be asleep halfway though one beer," I said. Sally's buoyant enthusiasm struck me as foreign as a Disney character in a cemetery, but I was happy to have it, countering the gravity of the trip and the tension with Ned.

We shared a bit of our story with Jamie. The guides knew, of course, about the attack last year.

"You're on a sacred journey," he said. "When tragedy comes into your life, the most beautiful thing you can do is to keep moving forward."

I smiled at him, grateful for his recognition of the importance of this odyssey. In my determination to get on the river, I hadn't realized how much I needed this validation.

It was a sacred journey. A pilgrimage. But surely it was not only about a river. The river flowed by, running, always running. I wanted it to stop. I wanted it to flow in reverse. I wanted there to be a dam in the river somewhere far back in the mountains, a lake to catch the water and keep it safe for swimming, for drinking, for watching sunlight dancing on the surface of still waters.

But the water flowed mercilessly north. There was healing in the tyranny, and tyranny in the healing.

I pulled out the plastic map case and extracted the maps carefully from the velcroed top.

"It looks like the first couple of days here are pretty straightforward. That's Kokotuk Creek across from us now." I pointed to the valley across the river from us and the corresponding line on the map. "And then we get to Esetuk Creek and the canyon on the third or fourth day — right here." I pointed to the place on one of the map sheets where the contour lines bunched together. "Those are the only serious rapids — we think. Is that right?" I felt pretty confident of our route, but it seemed worthwhile to talk it through with a guide.

"Sounds right," said Jamie. He took the next map sheet from me and ran his finger north along the braids of river. "Then you're into the foothills, and pretty soon after that the coastal plain. Once you hit the plain, the river really starts braiding."

"We'd heard that," I said. Ned nodded and Sally looked on.

"You should be fine. Just try to stay in the main current. We always end up walking the rafts over gravel bars there, no matter which way we go. You will too."

"How many times have you been down this river?" Ned asked.

"I don't know, probably five or six," Jamie said. "I've been guiding with Karen a few years now."

"It seems from our dad's journal that the water was a lot lower last year," I said.

"It was," Jamie concurred. "A lot more work this time last year."

I looked down the line of the river from one map sheet to the next, following the marks I'd made indicating all of the campsites from Dad and Kathy's trip. One more day, and we would be close to where Dad and Kathy had called me on Father's Day, the last time I heard his voice. How could I have known that their brief visit to Seattle, in February last year, would be the last time I would see his face? February 10th at 7:30, according to Peter's calendar, Peter and I had dinner with Dad and Kathy at Sostanza, a northern Italian restaurant in Madison Park. I remember Dad holding Kathy's hand on the table, the low and intimate light. I remember friends of Peter's parents at the table behind us, and a fire in the fireplace. I remember ordering halibut cheeks with a light lemon sauce and capers. February 10. Four months and sixteen days before I heard that they were gone.

Dad had thought about coming down for my concert with a local choral group in May.

"Mom's coming for that one," I said awkwardly.

"Oh, well, that's great!" said Dad quickly. "I'll come to another one." Of course he wouldn't be able to, but how could we have known?

I remember in Dad's embrace I could feel the softness of his aging skin, something I'd noticed with increasing concern. And his voice. In moments of panic, I wondered how long I would be able to remember his face, his voice. I loved that voice. I missed that voice. Kathy's laugh. Her smile. How could I not look back?

"I don't want to die in some hospital somewhere," he'd declared once with eyes sparkling, standing in the living room at the cabin as the river flowed at the base of the bluff outside the log walls. "If I start getting old or sick, I'm just going to walk out into the mountains, fall into a crevasse, maybe let a bear get me, be out in nature."

"Dad!" I'd said, horrified. I could not have invented that conversation if I'd tried. We hadn't talked much about death. It hadn't been time. It was too early. But what did we know about timing?

For most of my life, not only Dad's statements but his admonitions carried an urgency, a kind of veiled but panicked perception of the perils and shortness of life. In later years that urgency seemed to ebb, because of either the slow wane of age or, maybe, a satisfaction that his children were making their own ways, combined with a softening and opening of his spirit appreciating the pleasures and beauty of his faith, his marriage and family, and of the natural world around him. I like to know that this opening had already begun in him, this tendency of the soul toward things beyond this life.

We left the group with a dinner invitation for the following evening and headed back to our tiny campsite upriver. We had decided to forego bear watch, given our proximity to the guided group. I crawled into my sleeping bag happy for the full night of sleep ahead, even in continuous daylight. Ned and I were each in our own tents, and Sally was in her bivvy sack, all surrounded by the wire of the bear fence. I pulled a T-shirt over my eyes to keep out the light and let the quiet *beep, beep* lull me out of consciousness.

CHAPTER 9

A CEASELESS RIVER

The flow of a river is ceaseless and its water is never the same.
—Kamo no Chomei, *Hojoki*

We planned to stay at the same campsite for another day and night, allowing time to hike up the rising terrain east of camp. A gentle valley cut into the mountains, allowing a slow climb of about a thousand feet, according to the maps, at which point we could hike through the mountains to Esetuk Glacier. The opportunity to head up the side of a mountain in the Arctic put me back into my element. We spread out across the hillside for better visibility, to avoid damaging the fragile tundra, and because walking on the tussocks made it hard to get into a rhythm, so we each enjoyed having plenty of space around us. My thoughts settled into the slow movement of my legs up the mountain.

Memories flowed more freely as blood coursed through my veins with increasing power and speed, thought lubricated by movement. Some were thoughts I'd rather have avoided. For example, this one: no one who knew Dad and Kathy had actually seen them dead. Why had I not asked that family be able to see Dad at the funeral home when his body was delivered? Since the bear had been at the site for at least ten hours after their deaths, I figured their bodies weren't in very good shape.

I had failed. I had allowed fear to take over, and missed not only my chance but my responsibility to see them. Other cultures prepare a body with meticulous care. In the Jewish tradition, the foundation for the Christian faith, a family carefully washes a body in a prescribed order, ending with the face and hands in tandem. Those parts of a person that identify them: faces, hands.

After the body is washed, someone stays with it until it is buried.

My faith tradition has done a terrible thing in losing these rituals surrounding death, which tell us so much about what we believe about the body and the soul. Without the guidance of such traditions, and with only terror at my inability to handle what I might see in those massacred bodies, I'd allowed the saccharine funeral home representative to do all the work.

I hadn't even thought to bring clothes to the funeral home until they called and asked; I had tried not to think about what might be in those caskets. I'd assumed clothes wouldn't be helpful. And then I picked out Kathy's khaki-colored suit and shoes and Dad's khaki pants and houndstooth blazer, along with his cranberry-colored tie with the little squares on it that I loved. They would have looked nice together dressed like that. I also brought an undershirt for Dad, and boxer shorts and brown shoes and brown socks. I brought hose for Kathy. I wished later I'd polished Dad's shoes.

The next day at the funeral home someone said, "Mr. Huffman looked very handsome." I felt my throat closing again. Why hadn't I seen Dad, at least? Why hadn't I stayed with their bodies, kept vigil? That was the last time; there would be no other opportunities. How had life so suddenly stolen my last chance?

A watery cloud bridging earth and heaven hung in the valleys a thousand feet above the river on either side. Just outside of camp, a caribou trotted seemingly from out of nowhere, skirting us by a safe distance. It seemed to have a place to go, moving steadily toward the northwest. I wondered where the rest of its herd was; it was exposed, in danger on its own. Even so, it had a perky optimism to its gait, power in those thin legs, head held high. Then it stopped, looking directly at me. His heart, a heart the Gwich'in believe is part human, because they believe their own hearts share his, pounded under quivering flanks. I smiled broadly at him. He looked back with eyes brown and wide. His eyes held the collective consciousness of his species, like a messenger from another world or perhaps from the wisdom of our shared world.

The caribou pranced out of sight on the tundra, seeming to melt into the rarefied air from which he had appeared, and we headed up the mountainside toward the cloud. A razor-sharp awareness of the topography and vegetation directed my eyes to any place where our presence might surprise an animal. The little draw just there, the rise in the small stand of willows — each prompted a minor diversion in one direction or another just to be sure we didn't surprise *ursa arctos horribilis*.

With a conflicted mix of anger and reverence, I had embarked on this trip believing that if we did come across a bear, it would know that it owed me one; it would leave us alone out of respect. Losing Dad and Kathy had sliced me to my core. Understanding that I had lost them because of the violent action of another being twisted the knife. Even so, I did not wish to harm any bear with the weapons we'd brought.

Wait. That isn't true. A part of me wanted to find that bear, or its progeny, hold up the shotgun, pull the trigger, feel the recoil, watch the bear crumple, thick brown fur matted with red, watch its eyes glaze and dull. A part of me wanted that, but it was a weak, thin part of me, afraid like a small child. And *that* bear was as dead as my dad, as dead as Kathy, killed as quickly and with as much intent.

The rest of me needed to know the bear, to understand it, as deeply as its animal act had cut me. I imagined an encounter with a bear, close, human face to bear face, in which his small eyes considered me with wisdom and compassion, and then he turned his muscled body and moved back into the wild. But this was lunacy. The wilderness and the bear would show me no sympathy.

∧

Bears appear in the oldest records of humankind. The Chauvet Cave, which sits in the Cirque d'Estre at the edge of the Ardèche River Gorge in France, is one example. The cave is dated at 32,000 radiocarbon years, or 35,000 calendar years. Vivid paintings and etchings of large animals cover the walls. Nearly two hundred bear skulls have been found throughout the cave, fifty-three in what has come to be known as the Skull Chamber. Scientists are still hesitant to claim that this ancient grouping of skulls indicates a bear cult, although it is the best of myriad examples of apparently careful and ceremonial placement of bear bones across northern Europe. Scientist Philippe Fosse, one of the world's preeminent cave bear researchers, spends a month a year at the Chauvet Cave, and believes that "predators played a very important role in human evolution." In the varied and multifarious relationship between humans and bears, this cave appears in all respects to be the foundation.[4]

When we consider any number of ancient and modern indigenous cultures, not to mention the ubiquitous presence of bears in our own culture, it is hard not to be intrigued by the evidence of our spiritual connection to this creature. Carl Jung once said that "there is a bear with glowing eyes deep in the heart of human consciousness." The Gwich'in believe that this spiritual connection includes the bear's awareness of thoughts and words. "You can't talk about bear," says Catherine Mitchell of the Gwich'in. "Our people say it can hear you." Other native cultures refer to bear only obliquely, calling it grandmother, grandfather, all familial terms of respect. I never would have that kind of understanding. But it seemed there must be more for me to learn.

I hoped that indigenous, and specifically Inupiat or Gwich'in, spirituality might offer a way to understand this connection to the wilderness that our culture does not have words to describe. Maybe those answers would be salve for my wounds.

The Inupiat are primarily ocean people and are more familiar with the polar bear, or *nanuk*. Grizzly and polar bear rarely interact (though changes in wild animal behavior because of warming trends in the Arctic have resulted in more frequent interaction and even interbreeding), so the interior Gwich'in are more familiar with grizzly, which they call *shih*. Though the Gwich'in call themselves the Caribou People and think of themselves as sharing part of the heart of the caribou, they hold bear in even higher esteem. "Our ancestors say that long ago animals on earth used to talk to one another and to humans. There were shamans who talked to animals. The animals warned people of how to protect themselves from animals," says Gwich'in elder Hannah Alexie. "Grizzly is the strongest animal of the north. I always have respect for grizzly bear. They are on their own out there. We were told not to interfere with animals, not to tease them. They are on their own, like we are on our own. Be careful when you go onto the land, be alert." Then she adds, "All things are from our Lord. We have to protect our animals, never take more than we can use. This is what our elders taught us."

The bear is central to religious beliefs in nearly every Arctic and northern boreal culture from ancient times to the present, with uncanny similarities of beliefs and practices even among peoples of disparate geographies. The cult of the bear and the "sending home" ceremony practiced by the Ainu of Japan continued as late as the 1930s. In this ceremony, the Ainu men brought a bear cub home to the village. The cub was raised according to strict protocol in a cage kept in the village, and then killed and consumed with extraordinary intricacy of ceremony. For the Ainu, the bear was an intercessor between humankind and the mountain gods. The sending home of the bear allowed the god to return to the home of the mountain gods and report on his time in the village, judging the villagers by the careful execution of the rite surrounding his death.

This ceremony is shared by the Sami of Scandinavia, the Gilyaks of Eastern Siberia, and the Inupiat and Gwich'in of North America. The hunt for a cub is conducted when the bear is denned in early spring, and meticulous instructions explain the use of the implement for killing the bear. Additional prescriptions detail the preparation and consumption of bear meat by a village, with specific gender restrictions. In the case of the Gwich'in, the skin is stretched, and the women preparing the skin must walk around it clockwise. Bones are separated at the joints, so that no bones are broken. Finally, the various cultures follow strict tradition with the ornamentation of the bear skull and special preparation of the bones in order to support the bear soul's journey back to the home of the gods.

Environmental historian Paul Shepard suggested that these ancient cultures believed that bear is tutor to man. "The human question went beyond 'How do we survive the cold winter?' to 'How do we survive the cold death?' The bear more than any other teacher gave an answer to the ultimate question — an astonishing, astounding, improbable answer, enacted rather than revealed ... the bear was master of renewal and the wheel of the seasons, of the knowledge of when to die and when to be reborn ... the bear seems to die, or to mimic death, and in that mimicry is the suggestion of a performance, a behavior intended to communicate."[5]

Shepard believed that the survival of the wilderness is key to the survival of the psyche of humankind. He contended that wilderness, and specifically the presence of and human coexistence with predators, and especially bears, which share habitat and omnivorous characteristics with humans, helped to form the psyche of *homo erectus* by teaching us to come together as communities to protect ourselves from predators. Grizzly expert Doug Peacock agrees that "a hundred thousand years of evolution bind our genome spiritually and psychologically to those ferocious beasts ... the anchor of the wild keeps us tethered. Somewhere in the modern psyche we crave contact."[6]

A tethering. A ferocity. This is the dichotomy I wrestled to hold in my mind, holding it gingerly away from my heart as it worked desperately to heal.

▲

There was a time when I thought I would be happy if I died. The past year, I'd wanted to die, wanted to stop the pain of grief. But another time, after my freshman year in college, I'd hiked alone in Hatcher Pass in the Talkeetna Mountains north of Anchorage with Oakley, our golden retriever. Granite ridgelines sliced the clear Alaska air, carving away extraneous thoughts. When I brought pictures from that hike to college the next year, one roommate, a debutante from Louisiana, gasped, "Oh my God! Is that *Switzerland*?" No, more vast. More wild. More beautiful.

I had not seen a soul on my hike, and heated by exertion, I stopped to let my head hang back, feeling my pulse pounding at my throat and the breeze, cool from the snowfields, warm from the sun, passing over my skin. Oakley and I scrambled up a scree slope and walked along a ridge, stopping to rest where we could look across the verdant valley under a cerulean sky. There was no water near, so I squirted water from a bike bottle into Oakley's mouth. He lapped it up appreciatively. A marmot whistle cut through the mountain air. Another answered from across the valley. I listened and thought I heard all the wisdom of the world. In sound and wind and light and blood, the pleasure I felt through every part of me could only be called erotic. I remember thinking that if I died, right there, right then, I would be happy with my life, and with my death. It was enough.

In these Arctic mountains, though, I wanted to suffer. I wanted to live, so that I could suffer, believing that if I was hurting more, I was somehow closer to Dad and Kathy, impossibly closer to the time of their deaths and thus closer to their lives. I wanted that pain, reaching for it with growing desperation in the moments it ebbed.

Even as we gained altitude, the ground remained boggy, and my spirits sagged. Because of permafrost, summer tundra is frequently soggy; there is nowhere for water to go. Arctic grasses grow clumped together, attracting and holding dust blown by the wind to build up peat around the base of the grass. This helps protect it in the deep freeze of winter, when icy blasts hurl frozen particles across the landscape. In the summer, though, the unwieldy tussocks foil foot placement, interrupting any rhythm of movement. Each step was a struggle. I put one foot in front of the other, ascending into cloud, driven only by hope and the familiarity of moving my legs up the side of a mountain.

Along the way a caribou antler, bleached white by the sun, contrasted sharply with the tundra. Both male and female caribou grow antlers and shed them every year, the females after calving, and the males after the fall rut. It seemed as good a spot as any to rest.

"You guys want to take a break?" I asked. "I could use a granola bar."

I sat on one of the drier tussocks, letting my daypack fall off my shoulders and pulling out a bag of granola bars and my Alaska wildflowers book. I handed bars to Sally and Ned.

Turning the pages in the book, I tried to identify the tiny blooms surrounding us. Despite my reference book, my attempts at classification were subject to a large margin of error: still, I could name the plentiful white mountain avens, capitate lousewort, yellow anemone, groundsel, frigid arnica, tall cottongrass, moss campion, Arctic sandwort, bell heather, woolly lousewort, and something I thought was either purple mountain saxifrage or Lapland rosebay, I wasn't sure.

"What's that?" Sally pointed to the top of the ridge one valley away from us. Two brown shapes made small by distance moved slowly toward the valley between us.

I squinted. "I don't know … Is that …"

"Are they bears?" Ned asked.

"I can't tell."

The three of us stood, willing our eyes to bring the shapes into focus.

"Might be. They're big," I said. "I don't think so. I think they're ... Wow."

"What?"

"I think they're moose. See that hump on their backs ... and their legs? Now that they're coming this way a little you can see their legs. That's really weird."

"I didn't think moose came so far north," Ned said.

"Yeah, I didn't either. Or so high on a mountain. Strange."

"Well, should we keep going?" asked Ned.

"We'd better if we want to get to the glacier," I said.

I tightened the straps of my daypack, and we all clambered to our feet.

"Did you and Dad ever talk about stuff that was really important?" I asked Ned. I watched my boots to keep from stumbling.

"Yeah, sure," he said.

"I mean, I know he wasn't great at having meaningful conversations, but once in a while he could surprise you," I said.

"He did a lot of telling me what I should do," Ned said.

"When I told him I was dating someone once," I said, "he asked me if that guy knew how to love me. That was a surprise."

Ned let out something like a snort. "Seriously? You and I definitely had different relationships with him."

"He really cared," I said. "I think he just didn't always know how to say it."

Ned seemed to pick up the pace then. I noted it but didn't try to match him. It occurred to me that in addition to mule-headed stubbornness and a love of reading, Ned and I also shared the need to make my father proud, and that in spite of, or perhaps because of, this similarity, we were less likely to bridge the gap between us.

With Ned moving farther ahead, I slowed down until Sally caught up. "Geesh, I can't believe the ground is still so wet this far up the mountain," I said.

"You mean this isn't normal?"

"Not where I'm used to hiking. But it's my first time here too. How are you doing?"

"It's hard work, but it's nice to walk for a change," she said. I watched her make her way one careful footstep at a time, in the manner of someone still learning her way. She was a good sport, pushing herself, never complaining.

"You guys aren't very close, are you?" she asked, with a care I found surprising and an awareness that startled me.

"No, we've never been close. I think we've always loved each other but never really got along."

"I never had a sibling," she said. "Always wanted one."

"Yeah, my youngest brother seems to bridge the gaps," I said. "But Ned—he's tough. I'm sure he thinks I am too. You're awfully good to come on this trip, given our reasons and our relationship. Guessing you didn't know much about either. Thanks for hanging in there."

"I'm just glad I was able to come," she said.

We finally reached the top of the first hill, where Ned was waiting. This far up the mountainside, the cloud wrapped us in a discomfiting gray, limiting visibility to tens of feet. A house-sized boulder perched atop the hill, the only thing visible. Ned was looking at the map. Getting to the glacier would require more than an hour of steady walking. Even with the most positive attitude, walking in soggy tussocks in the middle of a cloud isn't much fun.

"We won't get much farther in these conditions, and won't see anything even if we did," I said. "I'm okay with going back to camp if you guys are."

Ned nodded glumly. "Makes sense."

"Sorry, guys," I said. This trip, it seemed, would be all about conceding inadequacies.

"I'm glad we hiked anyway," said Sally, and I found myself grateful for her cheerfulness and ashamed of my discouragement.

"Let's have lunch and then head down," I said.

Ned already had his pack off. Sally and I followed suit. I laid the shotgun next to me pointing out into the cloud.

"Remember that time Dad took us up to camp at Williwaw Lakes and the tent blew down?" I asked Ned, pulling a sandwich out of the top pocket of my daypack.

"How'd that happen?" Sally asked.

"The wind was just too strong," I said. "It was one of those old tents with the center pole, and the pole ripped right through the top of the tent."

"It was something like two or three in the morning, wasn't it?" Ned asked.

"I just remember it was dark, but starting to get light again," I said, then laughed. "Sam and Max screamed. They were still pretty young. And it was scary, that tent whipping around like evil spirits had got ahold of it."

"And Dad ended up carrying Oakley in his pack on the way out."

"That's right." Oakley had run alongside us with exuberant joy the whole trip, cutting her paws on the sharp Chugach shale until they bled, blooms of blood trailing her in patches of snow. Dad had found a way to put her in his pack and carry her the rest of the way to the trailhead. A family headed in on the trail had stopped to snap a picture.

"Did you guys do a lot of camping?" Sally asked me.

"I guess so," I said. "It was just part of how our family, especially with Dad, spent time together. Camping, skiing, hiking, and for a while, running."

"Remember when Dad wrote us notes to get out of school to ski when Alyeska hosted the Junior Olympics?" Ned asked.

"I'd almost forgotten. He loved skiing. Maybe too much for a while."

"Why too much?" Sally asked.

"Well, one New Year's Day we skied all day and then night-skied. We were at the bottom of the mountain and there was an icy mogul field. He caught an edge and fell and separated his pelvis. He was in the hospital for a week and was supposed to lie low for a year."

" 'Supposed to' being the operative words," Ned said.

I nodded. "In March he put duct tape around his hips and went back out to ski again. Crazy!" I smiled at the memory. But I also remembered seeing Dad faint from pain in the hospital after separating his pelvis. He had been trying to use a walker on the way to the bathroom. Dad's mortality dawned on me that moment, an angry flush of terror. He was vulnerable, just like I was. Just like I'd thought he was not.

"We never did anything like that growing up," Sally said. "I bet it was fun."

"Well, in that case, you're pretty gutsy to make the Arctic your first big trip!" I said.

She smiled. "I figured, why not?"

We finished our lunches, took last swigs of water, and stood to head back down to camp.

Even going downhill required laborious effort, and that combined with our failure to meet our day's goal made me again doubt my intentions and the wisdom of our journey. I'd leapt into this trip with a wild abandon. It made no sense to have come here with Ned, whom I didn't trust, and another person I didn't know. It made no sense to head straight to the place Dad and Kathy had died, a place still sticky with blood and drenched in lost hopes.

At the same time, this wilderness that had at first looked featureless was beginning to bloom around me. Watching wildflowers and birds against lines of landscape and light, I fell under the spell of beauty and wildness and felt a growing awareness of place.

But my mountains were failing me. The clouds pressed down on us, and we slumped under the weight of darkness. I felt heavy and inadequate. My legs, fatigued, stumbled. I cursed under my breath and stopped to rest, sucking air into my lungs, feeling my heart pounding.

And then, descending, we broke out below the clouds. Sunlight spilled onto the landscape, pooling in the river far below, a shimmering silver ribbon traveling the valley. The glistening thread of Kokutuk Creek in the mountains opposite wound through low hills to join the sunlight in the Hulahula. Dark clouds deepened the greens and blues of the landscape to the depth of timelessness, a glimpse of the eternal. A benediction. It seemed to me then that learning to see would allow me to witness, which could teach me how to know both this unfolding creation and God.

I had a waking dream. I was an eagle, soaring in the high, thin air. Hope was an eagle too, and not far from me. We glided far above the ridgelines, catching the air currents. But I was unsure, and flew toward Hope. Hope took pity, and flew toward me. We raced together through thin blue sky, and joined our claws, and fell, hurtling through clouds and past mountaintops. I was afraid. I clung in desperation. If I did not let go, we would both die. In my terror, I clutched tighter. The mountainsides blurred. Could I release my claws and spread my wings? Would I?

This was my challenge. I didn't want to let go. I thought I was still in control. I didn't want to do the one thing that life demanded. I thought if I held on tightly enough, if it hurt enough, I could keep Dad and Kathy with me. I wouldn't have to acknowledge that they were gone. I could move toward their final campground and find them and hold them close. And even as my talons cramped into position, I felt the tearing away, and it hurt as much as the first pain, and I knew that if I did not break loose, I would be pulled down into that place called death and would not be able to return.

And still I needed to see. I needed to hear. I needed to know.

▲

We made it to camp just before a brief but determined down-pour and enjoyed short naps in our tents. As evening approached, Jamie walked toward us, inviting us to join the group downriver for dinner. We headed over to the considerably more comfortable setup the guides had rigged, including a cooking and eating tent made of mesh for mosquito protection. Karen and Jamie's years of outdoor cooking experience provided a dinner that even after a few days of dehydrated food seemed nothing less than gourmet. I was surprised that they cooked next to the eating tent, which was only a short stroll from the sleeping tents, and kept their food in plastic barrels, not bear cans. Maybe we really were overreacting with our precautions.

"We were just talking about the history and geology of the Arctic," Jamie said as we joined the rainsuit-clad clients in the mosquito tent.

"Thanks for letting us join y'all," I said, with a general smile toward the clients, their eager faces still bright with the newness of their trip.

"The Arctic as we know it used to be a part of a refugium, which is a place that was not covered in ice during the last ice age," Karen explained.

"That's kind of ironic," Sally said.

"It is, in some respects. A huge ice sheet covered much of North America, and glaciers carved deep into the Brooks Range, but this area of the Arctic north of the mountains was bare. That's one of the reasons there are so many remains found here of dinosaurs and ancient peoples."

"Can you explain the polygons we saw flying into Grasser's?" I asked.

Karen nodded toward Jamie.

"They're pretty cool," Jamie said. "The permafrost below the surface layer of earth can be up to a hundred thousand years old.

As the surface freezes and thaws, the expansion and contraction of land causes it to buckle. Have you heard of the naturalist named Pielou?"

I had, and several of the clients nodded. I guessed it had been on their suggested reading list.

"Well, she explains that tundra polygons form when the freezing earth cracks, contracting from extreme cold. In the spring, meltwater seeps into these cracks and freezes the next winter, forming an ice wedge. This process continues every year, and the ice wedges get bigger. As they grow, they push up soil on either side into a berm. Meltwater collects in the low centers in the spring. The soil is very different in the center from the soil on the ridges and the outside edges of the polygons, and supports very different plant life. This is what you see as polygons from above."

I was happy for the even meter of speech, the gentle flow of information that had nothing to do with bears, nothing to do with grief, nothing to do with fear. I sat back and listened, enjoying the low din of cooking and conversation around me, surprised that I seemed to crave companionship as much as solitude.

One of the clients on the trip, a silver-haired man in matching blue rain jacket and pants, asked about the political history of the Arctic. Karen responded. "The refuge was originally formed in 1960, though it was smaller then, just 8.9 million acres. Back then it was called the Alaska National Wildlife Range. In 1980, ANILCA — the Alaska National Interest Lands Conservation Act we've talked about before, which preserved more than a hundred million acres of Alaska for parks and refuges — renamed the area as the Arctic National Wildlife Refuge and increased the area to just more than nineteen million acres. But ANILCA also opened Area 1002 to further study." Karen pronounced 1002 as "ten-oh-two."

"1002 is named for the section of the law titled 'Arctic National Wildlife Refuge Coastal Plain Resource Assessment.' What we know as the coastal plain is the 1002. Despite strict timelines for completing the assessments, fifty years later the fate of the coastal plain is still undecided."

An attractive middle-aged woman from Texas in a red raincoat chimed in. "But you've been talking about how sensitive the area is. Why wouldn't it be protected?"

"Great question. I think it should, but there are still some people who want to develop, even though the chances of finding anything of value are slim. Money is a powerful motivator."

"What was it Jamie was saying about the compression of ecological zones?" someone else asked.

"The more we know, the more we understand how complex the land is and how little we actually know," Karen continued. "The refuge stretches from just east of the Prudhoe Bay oil development to the border of Canada's Yukon Territory, and from the northern coast to south of the Brooks Range. The Brooks Range reaches toward central Alaska in the west, but angles close to the coast in the east. The proximity of the range to the sea compresses several ecosystems into a very small space, making the Arctic Coastal Plain an area of remarkable biological diversity."

Jamie looked up from the stoves. "One hundred and thirty species of shorebirds migrate from every continent in the world to the Arctic each summer to breed and nest, and in the case of waterfowl, to molt. Many of these species travel thousands of miles without stopping."

The man in the blue rain suit shook his head in awe.

"You know that little bird we saw yesterday?" said Karen.

"The common redpole," the woman from Texas said eagerly, looking at her field notebook.

"Right, exactly. That little guy gains three times his body weight to make his migration. He almost can't get off the ground when he begins migrating. And the buff-breasted sandpipers come here all the way from Argentina," Karen said. "Northern wheatears

come from Africa and Asia, and tundra swans come from Chesa-
peake Bay."

Several people scribbled in their notebooks. I listened in appreciation. Even Sally and Ned were attentive.

"The Porcupine Caribou Herd we've talked about travels farther in its migration every year than any other terrestrial mam-
mal, up to three thousand miles a year, depending on their route.
They usually calve on the coastal plain, where they can avoid
predators and where the calcium content of the tundra is higher
than almost any other soil on earth."

"It's like Africa, but wilder!" the man in blue said.

"That's right, though, ironically, not as many people know of
or understand this wilderness," said Karen.

"So the caribou we saw yesterday was probably from that
herd?" asked another woman.

"Possibly, though there is also a smaller Central Arctic Herd
here that ranges from Prudhoe Bay to the Okpilak River," Karen
explained.

"We saw moose up on the ridgeline today," Ned said. "Is that
common? We didn't think we'd see them so high in the mountains,
or so far north."

"It didn't used to be so common," Karen said. "But the vegetation has really been affected by climate change, and now willows
are growing faster and farther north than they ever have. Moose
love willows, so they've come north too."

I was glad to learn more about the place into which I'd been
thrown by circumstance. It occurred to me then that I had a choice
about what I'd been given: to grit my teeth and try to muscle
through, or to train my wounded spirit to the possibility of wonder.
There was so much here I didn't know and didn't understand. So
much more beauty than I'd expected. I had much to learn.

Karen and Jamie served up a hearty chili with a green salad,
and we finished with apple cobbler made in a field Dutch oven.

The group regaled us with stories and thoughts about rivers and about travels in Alaska and other wild places, and we enjoyed easy conversation before retiring to our camp to sleep. The companionship of the wilderness girds the soul, but human companionship in the wilderness warms the heart.

Requiem

Offertorium

Adding the grace of music to the truth of doctrine ... we pluck the fruit of the words without realizing it.

—St. Basil, *Hom in Ps. I* (PG 29.211)

I'm squirming in my seat tonight. This rehearsal is painful. We're getting closer to performance, so we're into the details. Repeating passages again and again, trying to get the rhythm right, and the words. Nothing inspires me about being here right now. I'm not here because of Dad or Kathy, or because of beauty, or because of music or prayer. It is only the requirement of attendance that got me in my seat, on time, attentive.

More work with the men of the choir tonight, and I think of all the office work I still have to do when I get home before bed, things I need to have done before I go in to work in the morning. I don't have time to be here. And why do things I choose always have an element of discomfort? Who designed these chairs to be so uncomfortable? I take some solace in memories, which seems to be my new *modus operandi* on the other side of an event showing me life is a blend of not only present and future but the past too.

I'd spent hours in these folding chairs accompanying my dad to his opera choir rehearsals when I was a child.

Ʌ

Dad sang with the Anchorage Opera Chorus when I was young, occasionally singing short solo parts like the gatekeeper in *Rigoletto*. I remember the conductor as a woman of extreme talent and beauty. Her name was Elvira Voth. Pitying my attendance at Dad's rehearsals, perhaps, she gave me the task of writing down measures she wanted to revisit over the course of a rehearsal. I took my responsibility seriously, sitting on a hard metal seat just behind her, as single-mindedly intent as her choristers were. She spoke the measures to me over her shoulder as she continued conducting: measure 36, measure 141. I wrote them down dutifully.

We attended the free opera dress rehearsals as a family. I remember just before the storm scene in *Rigoletto* someone yelling up from the orchestra pit, "The bass drum! Can anyone find the bass drum?"

Dad's resonant voice supported melodies of praise at church for most of my growing-up. More than these formal performances, though, I remember him singing songs from *Fiddler on the Roof* in the car on the way to and from a small cabin north of Anchorage, singing arias and spirituals walking through the house, waking us up singing the military call "You've got to get up ..." or the old folk song "Lazy bones, sleeping in the sun ..." He sang into his deep laughter, and even if we were annoyed as kids, we always ended up laughing too.

Dad's laugh started deep and slow, suddenly erupting into prolonged musical interlude, his whole body convulsing, eyes crinkled shut, head back. It was the kind of laugh that came on like a tidal wave, a swell that swallowed the room in its exuberance. I remember him sitting at the head of the table one night after dinner, dishes cleared, and reading to us "The Ransom of Red Chief" by O. Henry. He laughed so hard tears ran down his cheeks and he had to steady himself against the table to keep from falling over. I didn't have to understand what was so funny; his laugh was its own entity.

When I was still in high school and starting to understand that a parent is someone you know only a part of, I went to coffee with my dad. Coffee shops were new then, and Café del Mundo on Northern Lights was our first haunt before Kaladi Brothers opened. It was a cold clear day in Anchorage, and a sheer covering of ice climbed up the windows of the coffee shop, sun glinting off of the ice crystals and spattering on the walls inside.

I asked Dad the awkward questions of someone becoming an adult talking to an adult, trying on this new relationship, not knowing how to make it work but wanting it to, trying to know myself through knowing him better. What would he do if he could do anything at all, and what would he change about his life if he could?

He was too tired to answer fully, and we were too new to this kind of adult conversation. "I think I might have pursued music more seriously," he said, and his soft brown eyes looked off into that ice-diffused sunlight somewhere I couldn't reach, and the music was there too, my dad and the music, hanging in that light.

I remember looking at him differently, this dad I idolized in many ways, seeing him as a person with dreams that sometimes got tangled up in life, seeing him with longings that went unfulfilled.

The same voice that laughed and sang also erupted in anger and frustration, with a volume and intensity matched to his physical size. His quick temper had been legendary in his younger days, both at home and at work. When I worked at his law firm as a receptionist one summer, a colleague of his, after a staff meeting, stomped through the lobby where I sat at the desk. He hesitated briefly, his eyes darting as though chased by his frustration, and blurted, "Your father ... is very ... passionate!" and continued on to his office. I wanted to laugh, because I knew it was true. I wanted to say, "Oh, you have no idea."

It wasn't Dad's temper that was hardest to deal with. That tended to be a flash in the pan, a momentary raising of the roof. It was directed. It was not unkind. Then it was over. He would come upstairs while I was still fuming and ask how things were going — which would, of course, make me even more furious. But what was hardest about Dad was his ceaseless judgment of himself and, by extension, us. "He always thought of himself as that Kansas farm-boy," one of his office colleagues said, referring to Dad's wrestling with the various elements of his nature. Within the span of one conversation, Dad would marvel at the daring of a paraglider, and then say, "Those guys wouldn't have the guts to start their own business." It was a proclivity that said more about his own father than himself, a feeling of never quite measuring up, one of those pieces of self that sticks to each following generation like gum to a shoe. When that trait appeared in my own life, I thought that it said more about him than it did me — until I grew up and had to accept that regardless of its origin, it was mine to work through.

The expectations Dad expressed were meant to help us over-come these insecurities, to see that we were better than any doubts we had about ourselves. I found myself unwilling to admit my own shortcomings to him. I wanted him to see that I'd met his expecta-tions. After I left for the army, I remember him asking several times, "How are things going? Do you need anything? You paying your bills okay? You'll let me know if you need any help, won't you?"

"Sure, Dad," I'd say, but I was more likely to take a second job flipping burgers than ask him for anything. The couple of times I ran short on cash, I called my brother Sam for a loan. Dad would have been hurt by this, but when I held up my understanding of his expectations against my role as daughter, I paid more attention to his expectations.

If passion and music go hand in hand, maybe it makes sense that so many of my childhood memories had to do with music: sitting at the piano in countless recitals, braids hanging down my back; playing the cello at our dining room table; singing in a sixth-grade musical; going with Dad to sing with the children's choir in the Anchorage Opera. I sang with the Chorale and Chamber Choir at

Duke, rushing to rehearsals after my ROTC lab in the woods, one time arriving still wearing camouflage paint on my face in order to be there on time. Music was always a part of my life, and I never thought much about it until I was older. Listening to and performing music helped me express passions and yearnings within community in a way I would not have known how to otherwise. Music was portable too; after college, I sang with choirs in the different communities where I lived during eight years in the army. The first piece of furniture I bought was a piano. On moving to Seattle, my first action after finding an apartment was to find and audition for a local choral group. When I went back to Alaska for Christmas, I sometimes sang in the St. Mary's choir with Dad and occasionally with Kathy. In a family in which talking about things that mattered was difficult, this musical connection between Dad and me bore a hieratic significance. Music was a steadfast friend in a turbulent life, resistant to passing time and changing circumstances. The tremor of a bow across a string, a chorus of voices, breath flowing across a reed — all echoed my own ache for connection through music and musicians, a need as deep as breathing.

So that's how I made it here tonight. Even at times when I don't feel it, I understand music's work in me, know it with an academic surety even when emotionally I am as dry as dust.

I suck down music as essence, as someone dying of thirst in the Sahara sucks down water. I gorge on it. Most of it runs off me like rains off parched soil. I can't keep it down. The sick rarely understand what they really need, or how much they can handle. All I know is that I crave it like a drug. When I signed up to audition for the Requiem, it seemed perfectly natural to hope for respite in the opportunity to sing. But this isn't respite. It is work, sometimes wonderful, sometimes wrenching.

Mozart's Requiem, like all Masses written to honor the dead, has been a favorite of mine since a class on music and poetry at Duke. The possibility of singing Mozart's Requiem with one of the greatest musicians of all time thrills me more than anything else I can imagine; it is the only thing inspiring imagination in a self that feels otherwise flat and dead. But somewhere inside of me I want it with everything I have, no matter how painful the rehearsal. Listening to the words again (and again!) as we work to get each sound and word right, I remember the liturgy I love. The Requiem combines the elements of this liturgy that supports, guides, and instructs me in worship I no longer understand with the music I crave. I need all the guidance I can get.

CHAPTER 10

A UNIQUE
OPPORTUNITY

When man finds that it is his destiny to suffer, he will have to accept
suffering as his task; his single and unique task. He will have to acknowledge that even in suffering he is unique and alone in the universe.
No one can relieve him of his suffering, or suffer in his place. His unique
opportunity lies in the way he bears his burden.

– Victor Frankl, *Man's Search for Meaning*

Certain winter mornings in Alaska, when the humidity is high
and temperatures low, ice crystals cling to the trees in a brilliant coating and rest suspended in the air like a bright veil. Time
is arrested until temperatures warm just enough for the crystals to
dissolve. Suffering is like this. The rest of the world is postponed.
Unlike the hanging crystals that inspire awe, however, suffering is
a jealous and lonely state. It can't abide the company of anything
else. It is greedy; it demands all of one's energies. It demands a
focus on absence and loss, and cleverly tricks one into believing
that there is no other possibility.

For two months in Alaska, I packed up and moved, donated, or
sold everything in my childhood home. Practical considerations
dictated efficiency: the difficulties of maintaining insurance on
an empty house, completing tasks from long distances, the sagging housing market. I think we all knew that to leave this home
required moving quickly, as is necessary any time one leaves a

place where memories, hopes, and dreams are buried deep. Our home was a two-story, open-floor-plan Northwestern style that, at the time it was built, was considered quite contemporary. The loft was open upstairs, with Sam's and my bedrooms on one side of the house, and Max and Ned's shared bedroom and the bathroom on the other. In between, the balcony looked down to the living room and the front hallway, and windows looked out to the trees, and the mountains and ocean to the west. The four of us had two primary tasks: emptying the house, and finishing the deck Dad had started. Sam, Max, and Ned stayed for a couple of weeks, and then came and went from Alaska as their work allowed. My boss had given me a blank check. I knew I needed to be there until things were completed. I also knew we needed to move with intention.

Just before Dad and Kathy's Hulahula trip, they had emailed photos of Dad in canvas work overalls driving a rented bulldozer, putting in concrete for the supports of a new deck off the dining room of our home. In the photo, Dad grins into the camera, happy to be doing work that allowed him to see and enjoy the results. He'd planned a large deck extending off the front of the house like the prow of a ship, out over the yard and toward the forest.

We had decided to finish the deck before selling the house. This wasn't a practical decision; each of us wanted — needed — to finish Dad's project, moving under separate but similar burdens of wanting somehow to make things right, not yet understanding that this was impossible, that there were some things that could not be made right in any of the ways we then understood.

None of us were carpenters, even avocationally. Among us, we didn't have the skills to do what Dad had begun or the energy to figure it out. So we found a carpenter who did most of the work, and he kindly obliged our desire to play a small part. The carpenter showed me how to force the boards into straight lines with one tool while nailing them down with another. Even lumber, made for straight clean lines, needed help to fulfill its purpose.

Along with the photos of Dad came pictures of two small dogs he and Kathy had taken home and considered adopting. He wrote the emails from the dogs' point of view. "What do you think of these people we're considering adopting?" I thought all concerned were great. Dad and Kathy decided at the last minute not to keep the dogs. They still liked to travel often enough that new pets would have been too difficult. I was glad for the dogs that Dad and Kathy had made the decision they did.

Someone suggested hiring someone to clean out the house. The idea nauseated me. No stranger would walk through the house to box up spices and toothpaste and books. Books, especially.

Books were things we had shared most next to music in our home, by reading and by way of gifts. Dad frequently gave as Christmas gifts books he had discovered the previous year: Neruda, Borges, a book on the nature of God. One distant family member went through the house and indicated piles of books he was interested in. I tried to disregard the intrusion and ignored the request. Dad's books stayed with us.

The books on Dad's bedside table were all books I had loaned him during his February visit or given him before: three books of Greek plays, a book on Tolkien, and *Peace Like a River* by Leif Enger. The last book was dog-eared a third of the way through. Knowing that our eyes had wandered the same pages, our minds had followed the same story, brought Dad back as though our minds could walk the same place together again if they chose. And it was an appropriate story too: a father in the Midwest and his children, smiling in the face of pain. A father who gave his life for his children. A father who crossed a river, and a child realizing it wasn't yet time to join him.

Did you like these, Dad? What did you get out of them? We never talked about them.

Dad's bedside-table books — into a box to come home with me.

We sorted clothes, filling boxes and carloads for Goodwill,

starting other boxes for ourselves. Kathy and I wore the same size and had frequently shared clothes. Sometimes, at the urging of my dad, who worried that I didn't spend enough money or time on my clothes, she bought me the same clothes she bought for herself.

I put two of Dad's suits into a box to be sent to me. I'm not sure why. They hung in my closet for the next six years.

For goodness' sake, he would have said. *Give them to someone who needs them. I don't need them now.* He's laughing, because he is now in a place filled with joy. *You can't imagine, Shan, it's beautiful.*

I need to keep these, Dad. I want them. I promise I'll give them away when I'm ready.

We donated the ping-pong table in the garage and other sports equipment to Alaska Children's Services, where Dad had done pro-bono legal work for years. He had a soft place in his heart for kids who grew up without opportunity, and had schemed many times about starting a school, maybe on a farm — with ponies! — to help them. He'd talked about the pony farm for grandchildren too. I don't know where the pony idea came from, or where he would have built it, but his plans abounded.

I packed up my room. Kathy had redecorated it when she and Dad overhauled the house ten years before. I'd spent the first night home from college at Christmas in tears. My room was no longer *my* room. Life had moved forward without me. Along with her sewing supplies, my varsity letter jacket from swimming and debate hung in the closet. I packed it into a box for Seattle. Kathy had framed and hung a couple of watercolors I'd painted when I was twelve. One was a doll leaning against a shelf of books. The other showed waves breaking against rocks where a lighthouse stood. I packed those too.

Then there was the attic, a plywood, windowless room lit by bare bulbs and filled with boxes from thirty years of my family's life. It was accessed by a hobbit-sized door off Sam's room.

I entered with trepidation—no, dread. It was a storage shed of memories, some long forgotten, ready to spring like a jack-in-the-box at any moment. It smelled of old cardboard, plywood, and dust. The bulbs shone like interrogation lights, exposing memories naked and cold.

The process was this: sort and pack in the attic, and then deliver to the garage. Sam had divided things up in the garage depending on where they were to be shipped. I tried not to get too involved in any particular box. It was impossible.

One box opened to a stack of soccer pictures. Me at ten: bobbed brown hair, an orange team T-shirt, and a broad gap-toothed smile. I remembered playing fullback and wilting from the charges downfield from one aggressive forward. Then she scored. Dad asked, Why don't you just charge back at her? He asked it with a smile. The next game I did. How could I not? I wanted only to make my dad proud. Sprinting toward each other, she and I collided at full speed. We fell flat on the wet grassy field. The screaming parents on the sidelines hushed, stopped moving, before resuming their din. She never charged my side of the field again. I think of that story as defining the person I became.

Were you proud of me, Dad?

Boxes of files—to be read or shredded.

Underneath a pile of papers, I found a plaque with a brassy musical note on it, an eighth note with a flourished tail. I'd won it at a piano competition in junior high. I played Grieg and something else I don't remember. I tied for first, and back at home after the competition, Dad said, "You didn't deserve to win. You didn't practice enough." I was mad. I knew he was right.

Later I bragged about that story, proud of Dad's challenge to me. Kathy gasped in disappointment. "Rich! I can't believe you'd say something like that!" Dad, embarrassed, denied it.

Boxes of paperback books—to Goodwill.

In another box, I found a Farm Bureau Insurance hat and a

couple of magic tricks from Grandpa Huffman from one of our visits to my grandparents in Topeka, Kansas. A small case with a black ball that seemed to disappear and a small wooden replica of an outhouse rigged with a mousetrap so that the walls exploded when you opened the door. I remember learning on those visits to Kansas that in case of tornado, we should go to the basement. The sky would get yellow, I heard. The funnel of a tornado twisted and curved and destroyed everything in its path. The idea terrified me. We didn't have tornadoes in Alaska. ("We don't have bears in Kansas is all I know," said my aunt.) The hat went into the Goodwill box. I kept the magic tricks. At this point I would take any magic I could get.

Boxes of elementary school papers and certificates, labeled with my name and put aside.

One day in the attic, I sat sorting books, my old school notebooks, files. I came across boxes of my diaries and boxes of correspondence. The idea of going through them seemed impossible. I put them in the Keep pile. There would be time later to sort these things.

In one instant the attic walls pressed in on me, the air stuffy, hot, oppressive. I set down the box I was working on and got up so quickly I had to steady myself against the wall, bumping my head on the angled ceiling. Still holding the wall, I walked out to Sam's room. The world wavered back into focus in the daylight and fresh air. I took a long, deep breath. I couldn't get enough air. I walked into my room. That little corner room used to make me feel so safe, both enclosing me and connecting me to the outdoors. But even the familiar had moved on. Now soulless brown boxes sat open, vacuous, restless, needing to be filled, needing to be closed, needing to be moved. I swallowed against a throat that had petrified.

I walked across to Ned's room, where Sam was working. The upstairs loft was open to the first floor on two sides and framed with windows, looking out at trees. The trees helped me breathe. Ned's room had few boxes left. Other than the furniture, it sat empty. The walls were bare. The bed was stripped. Sam pulled the last box off the walk-in closet shelf and set it by the bed. The only things left hanging in the closet were Dad's button-up shirts, a rod full of them. Sam reached for a handful of hangers.

"Can you — can you leave that for now?" I asked. My voice startled me. The question seemed to have come of its own accord. Sam removed his hand wordlessly. "Just leave them," I said. "I'll take care of the rest of the closet. Just ... let them be."

"Sure," Sam said. "I need to take a load down to Goodwill anyway." He picked up the remaining boxes and walked downstairs. I heard the garage door squeak open and slam shut behind him. A rumble from a diesel engine, fading away as the truck pulled out of the driveway. The house was silent. Through the open sliding glass door blew the scent of pine and the scattered chirps of chickadees on the cool afternoon air. I walked back out to the family room. Boxes of books sat mute in front of empty bookcases. Then I walked back to the closet of shirts.

Walking into the closet, I tried to sneak past any threatening memories. My hand reached out of its own accord. I felt the soft cotton. The rows of shirts were silent. Blue, white, and blue-and-white-striped shirts. The quietness seemed to echo, muffled in those shirts, murmuring memories.

I put my face in among them. I breathed in as deeply as I could, embarrassed, even though alone. I suppose they smelled like shirts. Laundered. Or dry-cleaned. Perhaps worn once or twice. They were memories. They were casings. They were shrouds. They were straightjackets. They were vestments. They were relics. They were the certitude of each day of my life before June 25. They had housed expectations. They were embraces. How many of those shirts had hugged me after I'd come home? How many of those long sleeves had circled me at five years old after playing the piano, at twelve after a swim meet, at nineteen coming home from college, at twenty-four coming home from the army? I grabbed the cloth in my hands, and it crumpled softly in my fists. Silence surrounded and scared me. This touching, this smelling of shirts. I did this for a half hour, maybe more.

Then with some resolve born of need and necessity, from some place deeper than I knew, I took an armful of shirts. A huge armful, too many to handle. I wiggled the hangers off of the rod with my body against them. I walked slowly out of the room.

The vortex started. I was nowhere close to a basement. There was nowhere to take shelter.

I made it two steps. Stumbling, I leaned against the balcony trying to breathe, my throat constricting. I held onto those shirts with both arms, tightly, and closed my eyes, and breathed, deeply, slowly. I opened my eyes and focused on the birch tree just outside the window, on the white papery bark peeling back in a graceful curve. The leaves were darkening to their summer greens. The sky was a blue so gentle it might have been a comfort. I took another breath and walked down the first flight of stairs. Just to where they turned to finish the journey to the first floor. And then my legs gave way and I slid, hard and slow, down the corner where the walls met. With the armful of shirts in my lap, I sat and cried. I cried like I cried when I watched the coffins descend. I cried like I can't remember ever crying since. My arms lost their strength, and I leaned into those shirts. I screamed, again and again and again until my voice stopped and the shirts took each of those screams into their softness.

∧

I graduated college around the time of the advent of email, so letters and the occasional phone call still served as primary forms of communication. I am grateful for this now, the physical substance and weight of letters, even if the physicality of cards is a sad surrogate for touching a hand. I think of how our atoms must intermingle, the sender and receiver, how there is an intimacy in this paper, and then I think how I put too much on things. The birthday cards included notes and greetings from both Dad and Kathy; letters came mostly from Dad. Each show early attempts at connecting with a child in evolving stages of life and increasing independence, attempts that even then sometimes felt awkward and yet which I appreciated and stored for the earnest and loving gestures they were. Some of these efforts seem silly now: "Are you following the NBA playoffs at all?" (I never had.) Mention of work he and Kathy were doing around the house or at church. ("We cleaned the windows at church yesterday. They were really nice. You can help this summer.") Several included cautionary comments on finances ("Our resources are low"), and all included some praise and admonition and sometimes points of edification. Most were followed by a P.S. ("What do you think about the Wellesley women protesting the invitation to Barbara Bush to speak? I'll be interested in your thoughts.")

On my first trip away from home to a music camp in Colorado when I was twelve, Dad wrote with concern that he'd forgotten to tell me how to get my bags from baggage claim. College letters ranged from three sides of a notecard to ten pages of yellow legal paper. On one he left a pink Post-it Note "P.S. word of the day: efficacious. Look it up! Or ... (over)" and he included the definition on the back. On another he drew out the settings on the table and described table etiquette.

While I was in the army's Airborne School in Fort Benning, Georgia, after my freshman year of college, he wrote, "Don't worry about the screamers—that's what they get paid to do. But you'd better respond smartly—that's what you get paid to do!"

One letter he began on a Friday and finished on Monday morning: "I just started a new book by William Dean Howell ... I am quite taken by his writing." He updated me on the boys and the weekend's plans, then finished his letter Monday morning from a table at Kaladi Brothers Coffee, where he'd driven to pay for Kathy's coffee because she had forgotten her purse. He described all he had to do at the office, then reflected:

> After doing this for twenty-three years, I continue to like it and continue to be amazed how much of success depends on just keeping it together—when one person falters, giving encouragement and support or connection; when another falters doing the same and so on. In other words, it is not brilliance (though that would be nice) that counts as much as it is tenacity and a certain "chutzpah," assuming, of course, at least better than average material to work with. I would add, I think creativity and flashes of brilliance can be—are—helpful but they are useless without the consistent, high degree of excellence displayed in everyday, year-after-year follow-through.... Incidentally, isn't it amazing what is happening in what is now the Union of Soviet States?

He continued for another page. Like most of his letters, it felt like conversation. Those conversations were sometimes easy, other times difficult.

"I am very excited for you and your opportunity to climb Mount McKinley," he wrote in a note he handed to me to take on the mountain.

> This is a chance for you to get a really good idea of what you're made of (I already know!) and to understand human relationships, different reactions of people when you're all pushed to the limit ... keep your wits on the most humdrum details. Where your clothes are, where you are, whether you're roped up, drinking water, etc. Paying attention to the drudgery and the details makes for safety—yours and the others'. You are younger but you've got a good mind and good instincts. Trust them where safety is concerned. Never hurry!! *Drink water and eat. Stay on the rope. Keep your clothes dry!!* We love you and are thrilled for you.

There were the hard times too, as I mentioned. In one letter when I was at college, Dad wrote, "I've been worrying that I haven't been telling you how proud I am of you ... I worry about the fact that you and I always seem to get in a shouting match ... I suppose it's partly to do with the fact that we're both strong personalities, partly my reluctance to let go, as a parent, and partly your natural tendency to become more independent. Whatever, it does not reflect on my basic trust and respect for you."

After our Christmas argument about the photo on the counter:

> I want to thank you for the gift of frankness which you gave to me ... I love you dearly, daughter. I hope you always remember that. I remember your birth, your infancy, your childhood, adolescence, teen years — so well.... You are at your core, a *fine* woman. You are blessed with God-given talent.

> Shannon, I can only encourage you to live your life fully. Live it within the restraints that are essential, tidiness, financial order, most of all, live it in a moral and loving manner. If you fail, start over and do better! Don't give up on yourself. There will be failures — every one of us has them, but don't give up on yourself or lose respect for yourself. Make your life one of high principles and high standards and strive to uphold them.

Each letter was written with an abiding awareness of things he'd wished he'd known, but hadn't, of life's fragility, of his desire to spare me the worst of it, as though he was suddenly, fiercely aware of the passage of time and how much more he wanted to impart. As though he hadn't been ready to let go, even while he encouraged me to fly.

This was my foundation. This was my guidance. This was my light. And now it was gone.

CHAPTER 11

BITTER RIVER

Return, return to your chalice of snow, bitter river,
return, return to your chalice of spacious frost ...!
–Pablo Neruda, *Canto General*

I flattened the map against a rock with one hand and held my
bowl of oatmeal in the other. A mug of Market Spice tea balanced on a rock next to me. It was ten o'clock. We were lagging
far behind the sun's steep ascent into the day. Dark curtains of
rain still hung heavily over the mountains and in the valleys, but
it was dry on the river. Looking at the markings I'd made on the
map, I determined that today we would make it to the Father's
Day camp, the camp where Dad and Kathy had talked and laughed
with me on the sat phone last year, the last time I heard their
voices. Today was also June 25th, the day the police declared Dad
and Kathy dead.

In the Jewish tradition, today would end a year of mourning.
There is a time to mourn, and there is a time to rejoin life. I was
supposed to be past the mourning period. It didn't feel that simple.
I suppose it never is. I'd had the Requiem. And I had this trip. I
had to understand that nothing would ever be enough. The idea
of a Kaddish is a prayer glorifying God. In the midst of life. In
the midst of pain. All of us who believe in God are supposed to do
this impossible thing: to praise in the midst of crippling sorrow.

We pushed the raft into the water, and then Sally and Ned took their places in the bow and I took mine as captain in the stern, an arrangement we had been finding worked well. The river started to braid, but we stayed easily in the main channel. The mountains on either side began to look less dramatic, older, with softer edges. It was another warm day, and I tied the top of the dry suit around my waist, now wearing just a black tank top under my purple PFD, which had been Kathy's.

It struck me then, as it had so many times before and since, how little I knew this place. Our childhood exposure to *Wild Kingdom* introduced us to oceans and African savannas, but this great wild space in our own state was still mostly unknown then. I'd backpacked and camped around the world. But even today, only a few extreme adventurers and hunters venture this far in Alaska's wilderness. Now I was swallowed up by the landscape. The sweeping grandeur of Alaska's Arctic is partly a function of scale. But more, its expansiveness is all encompassing. The root of the word nature is *nascis*, meaning "to be born." In the Arctic, for the first time in my life, I was thrust into the beginnings of creation.

"There's our first aufeis!" I announced. Aufeis (German for "ice on top") was entirely new to me; I'd only read about it in Dad and Kathy's journals and briefly in books. As we'd prepared for the trip, aufeis was a looming and unknown quantity, unfamiliar to me from other outdoor travel and adventures I'd had. As with so much in life, its greatest terror lay in its mystery. The temperatures this year were warmer than those Dad and Kathy had encountered last year, and our first aufeis had already melted to only a thin ridge of horizontal ice overhanging the water on one side of the river; the rest of it, several feet thick, sat harmlessly on a gravel bank. We pulled over to investigate.

In the sun, water drained off the ice, in some places a slow drip, and in others a steady stream, as the ice changed form to join forces with the river. Horizontal blue stripes on the ice indicated each layer of freeze, and a blue glow shone from beneath the ice sitting resigned on the gravel bar. Now that we'd actually come upon this unknown, our apprehension drained away, and we were able to see its beauty too.

Two sandpipers on the river's edge moved on their long legs with a desperate determination and feather-light jerkiness. Their goofy movements made me smile; the birds were so small against the backdrop of slabs of ice, the river, the mountains. They brought comic relief from the focus that was starting to take its toll, seeming to want to remind me that however grand the stage, life suggests a sense of humor.

We launched the raft back into the river. Multiple channels opened up as the valley widened. Many times it was hard to tell which was the primary channel; they all seemed similar. The way was not clear.

In a gentle section of river, the raft crunched to a stop on a gravel bar, a smooth and quiet arrest, but just as final. Ned and Sally jumped out and grabbed the rope around the top of the raft. I sat in the back, smiling at the sight of two people walking in the middle of a river, pulling a raft meant to float. By the third time that we ran aground, and all of us had to pull, it was less amusing, but there was nothing else to be done. Floating a large, heavy raft on this river, shallow even at high water, required creativity in both navigation and propulsion. I took some comfort in knowing that the guided group had similar rafts and would have to pull theirs too, and I tried to enjoy my first time walking in the middle of an Arctic river.

"Isn't it strange we haven't seen much wildlife?" Sally asked.

"I don't think so. The wildlife here have such extensive ranges, there's no way to tell whether you'll see something or not," Ned said.

"Even if we haven't seen much, you can be sure there are animals watching us," I said.

We pulled the raft back into the current as the river deepened again, though never without an abundance of rocks either just submerged or protruding from the river. While their visibility varied, their threat to the raft was similar. The rocks we couldn't see posed the biggest threat.

"Looks like a rapid ahead!" Sally said.

"Let's get out and scout," suggested Ned.

"Take out on the left?" I asked. "Paddle right!"

We paddled strong strokes toward the shore and I did a strong back-paddle to turn the boat upriver. Ned jumped out and pulled the raft onto the shore.

The three of us walked downriver, surveying the rapid.

"Not bad," Sally said. "Maybe a two, two plus?"

"Probably," Ned said. "We're going to head straight through the rocks in the middle of the river," he said, pointing, "and then go right. Looks like there's a hole just in the middle."

"Great," I said. "Looks like fun!"

"You know, you could name this rapids after your dad," Sally suggested. "I mean, it's the first real rapids we've hit."

"I like it. How do you do that?"

"Just write down the GPS coordinates at the top and bottom and a description, and then try to get it used commonly," she said.

"I'll get the top coordinates," Ned said.

We got back in the boat and pushed off. "We're going to want some speed," Ned warned.

"Paddle both!" I yelled.

Ned and Sally both dug in with their paddles. I paddled from the stern, alternating sides and using my whole back to pull on the paddle. "Keep it up!"

The raft surged forward. We passed rocks on both sides of us, staying to the center of the river, and then hit a wave train. I grinned as the raft bucked up and down, wedging my feet under the back seat tube of the raft to stay secure, letting my butt bounce off the rear of the raft. The main channel pulled us to the left around the corner, and we steered to the right of a rock fence on the left, then cut right to avoid a hole at the bottom.

"Whoo hoo!" I yelled. "Take out on the right, paddle left!" I back-paddled right and the raft swung into the eddy.

We got out to mark the ending coordinates, and I made the journal entry:

"Rich's Rapids" (rafts)

beginning coordinates: N   W
at high water: start center, pass small rocks right and left.
1st drop: follow wave train down middle, stay center around corner. Left after sand bar before "walrus" rock.
2d drop: follow left-most chute.
last drop: watch rock fence to left. Cut left below rocks. Pass over to right.
Ending coordinates: N   W. Ending elevation 1752'.

Looking back, I'm embarrassed we considered naming something wild after any person. Better to do as the Native Americans did: name something by its inspiration. Denali, "the great one" — not McKinley, the name of a president who never set eyes on its icy peaks. In New Zealand, the English names for natural features are often the names of white explorers. But the native Maori words suggest the spirit of the place. The rapids we passed should remain nameless, carrying the more substantive — and lighter — weight of the wind and rain, the snow, and the sighs of the Arctic.

This, it now seems to me, is a difference between people *of* the land, and people *on* the land, between humility and hubris. It is why a part of our Western culture looks with envy at indigenous people's beliefs: they come from a deeper wisdom of themselves and their world than we can hope to reclaim. We envy this, while ignoring the potential of this wisdom in the name of supposed progress, even as such progress continues to erode that wisdom or the possibility of our ever recovering it.

It is too hard to try to change our inadequacies. I began to learn, from this trip, a sense of relief in the world's largeness, that creation has the power to heal both us and itself—if we understand it as creation. The Arctic revealed itself as desert, vast and intricate with the openness of both great innocence and great wisdom. Emerson once wrote that "beauty in nature is not ultimate. It is the herald of inward and eternal beauty ... The happiest man is he who learns from nature the lesson of worship." I still had much to learn.

Below the rapids the river coalesced into one current again, and the raft moved easily on the smooth waters. Just a few minutes downriver, on the left, a wide, inviting valley led back into the mountains. A creek spilled out of the valley. Kotuk Creek. A gentle gravel bar bordered the river.

"Should we take a breather?" I asked.

"Sure," Sally said.

"How about the gravel bar straight ahead?" We pulled into a small take-out on the tip of an island sitting midriver. Ned and Sally got up to stretch their legs. I pulled out the map, and then I saw it. I hadn't been paying attention. Looking across the river into the valley, the rise and fall of the hills leading to the mountains corresponded to the contour lines on the map, and the rocky beach just below it was the campsite.

"This is the Father's Day site, just across the river," I said.

Ned walked away and up the beach without a word. Sally opened her daypack and found a granola bar. I picked out a rock to sit on and looked across the river. Dark clouds hung low in the mountain valley, resting comfortably, stable.

Last Father's Day in Seattle, I had known Dad and Kathy would call. It was their planned call from the river, so that we could connect on Father's Day. I had told them that I would be hiking that weekend, and asked them to call in the evening so that I wouldn't miss the chance to say hello.

I woke up that Sunday morning on the shore of a sparkling alpine lake, one of several tucked into a craggy cirque in the Central Cascades in the Alpine Lakes area. I had hiked into Rampart Lakes with a small group of friends, including two new friends from New Zealand, Alex and Katharine, who had recently relocated to Seattle for work.

The night before, our new Kiwi friends had been nervous about the nightly ritual of hanging our food fifty yards away from our campsite, since we were in black bear country. I had laughed and said, "Anyone have anything else? Toothpaste, granola bars?" Alex and Katharine peered out of their tent, which they'd set up in the middle of our small group so they would have plenty of warning if there was an unexpected intruder. "Really," I said, "bears don't bother you. They want less to do with you than you want to do with them. We just hang up the food so they aren't tempted to get too close."

"In New Zealand, we don't have anything like this to worry about," Katharine said. "I like it better that way. The worst thing is the Keas stealing your bootlaces."

"Don't worry, really," I said. "I've been backpacking my whole life, and I've never *seen* a bear except from the car or in a zoo. You just have to be careful."

"Well, make sure you scream nice and loud if one comes into camp, so we have plenty of warning!" Alex said, zipping the two of them into their tent.

Peter had not come on that weekend trip. Things weren't going well between us.

"I just don't feel like I can make it," he'd said. "Work's really busy."

"Okay, well, I'll miss you," I'd said, trying to hide my disappointment and the feeling that our relationship was decaying. "But I really want to go. If you're going to be busy, we'll make sure we're back in plenty of time for me to help with dinner on Sunday."

It was so much nicer to be in wilderness with him. We shared a fierce love for wild spaces, close to home or far away, desert or mountains, arctic or tropical. As long as the space was natural, it nourished our souls.

Peter and I met in business school at Dartmouth. He had taken two years off to work for a start-up between his first and second year, an atypical academic path, so he returned to a cohort he had not met. Our class size was among the smallest among business schools, so classes could be tight, even cliquish. While at an internship in Minneapolis over the summer, a woman from his first-year class and I met at a party in the heavy summer air. "Watch for Peter Polson," she said. "He's joining your class this year and won't know anybody. He's really outdoorsy — loves hiking and skiing. He's a really good person too. You can't miss him. He's six and a half feet tall and has a huge smile."

We met early on. Both of us were dating other people, but I could not get him out of my mind. He seemed to be the serious type. I figured he was as good as married. Peter joined our small group of avid hikers, backpackers, and skiers. Our first hike together was up Franconia Ridge in northern New Hampshire. The weather forecast deteriorated to rain and slush, even at lower altitudes in Hanover, and all but the German exchange student begged out of the hike.

The three of us hiked up a steep, forested trail, breaking out onto a bare ridgeline. Rain turned to whiteout conditions. The wind howled. I cinched my hood around my freezing chin, squinting into the gale, and carefully extracted the map from my pack, trying to keep the wind from ripping it from my gloved hands.

"Which way?" I yelled through the wind. Peter pulled out a compass.

"Looks like we are here," he said, pointing at the map, "and the trail will go ..." The compass needle vibrated tremulously. "Back just behind us and to the right." We snapped a picture in the howling gale and, with the help of Peter's compass, picked our way back to the trail descending the ridge. It was the first of many times we would work together to find the way.

The company I accepted an offer from sent me to Seattle after graduation. Peter was a Seattle native who was also returning to work in his native city and recommended great neighborhoods to look for apartments. Halfway into my first year in Seattle, I told a good friend, "I know this sounds crazy, since we aren't even dating, but I think I'm going to marry Peter."

A year after moving to Seattle, both of us still single, we started dating. I had never before met someone I thought I'd marry. I was smitten.

We had a good time, but not good enough. Things were fine, but not better than fine. It wasn't what either of us wanted for our lives. No matter, I thought. We'll figure it out. We are meant to be together.

Coming back from the hike on Father's Day, I called Peter to let him know I was on my way. Then I checked my voicemail.

"Hi, Shannon, it's Dad and Kathy," the message said. "Sorry we missed you today! We'll try you later if we get a chance. We love you!" I was frustrated that they had called early. I didn't want to miss my chance to talk to them. Before they left on these trips, Kathy would email and remind us that they'd be on the river over Father's Day in case we wanted to send a card early, addressed to her, so she could bring it along as a surprise. I'd sent my card out in time, but had planned to put pictures in a travel mug to send along as well and hadn't finished the mug.

Back in Seattle, Peter grilled salmon on the deck under the wisteria. His parents, as well as his sister and her family, joined us around the picnic table in the easy summer air. I had my phone next to me in case Dad and Kathy called again, feeling guilty for being tied to technology during a family dinner, but not wanting to miss a call. We finished dinner, and still they hadn't called. I felt just a bit desperate. I couldn't call the sat phone, since they turned it off when not in use to save batteries and kept it in a watertight case. We cleared the table. Peter's family left.

Minutes later, the phone rang. "Hi, Shannon?" The phone crackled just a bit, but was surprisingly clear for satellite connection.

"Hi, Dad!" I said. I grinned with selfish relief. "How are you doing up there?"

"Oh, we're just having a great trip," he said, a satisfied chuckle in his voice. "How are you?"

"We're great. Just had grilled salmon with Peter's family. Happy Father's Day, by the way!"

"Thanks! You have a good hiking trip?" Dad was always asking us about our lives, and I wanted to hear about their trip!

"It was great, Dad, really pretty. How's the river?"

He laughed his deep, belly laugh. "We're having a great time! Let me put Kathy on!"

"Hi, Kathy! How's the trip?"

"It's just beautiful. Your dad had a spill today, but everything was okay."

"What happened?" I was concerned. They were a long way from help.

"Oh, a piece of aufeis broke off and the wave flipped his kayak. He was just fine though."

"Well, that's good. What did you guys have for your Father's Day dinner?"

"Black beans and lentils. It was perfect!"

"That sounds great," I said. I smiled. It was good to hear their voices.

"Well, I'll put your dad back on," Kathy said.

"Great, good to talk to you. Have a great trip! I love you!"

"Love you too."

A brief pause as the sat phone was passed from one canvas chair to the other.

"Shan?"

"Hi, Dad. Sounds like you're having fun, though you left out flipping your kayak!"

He laughed again. "Oh, it all turned out okay. Nothing even got wet."

"Well, be careful up there," I said, feeling wistful, wishing I could give him a hug on this day honoring him.

"Did we tell you we saw a wolf?" His voice was easy, relaxed, and intensely happy.

"Really?"

"Actually, we saw two — a gray wolf our first day out, and a white wolf just this morning."

"That's amazing!"

"Just beautiful. Well, better let you go; this is two dollars a minute," he said.

"Okay, Dad. Happy Father's Day. I love you!"

"Love you too, kiddo."

That had been it, a quick call of only a few minutes. The river in the background, sand in their water bottles, life in their voices.

How do you know what word will be the last word? How do you know you should hold onto it, lock it away?

Three days later Peter and I broke up. Two days after that, I got the phone call from Kaktovik. Now a year had passed. Peter and I were friends; he had come with me to the funeral and supported me through the darkest year of my life. I invited him on the raft trip, hoping he would come, knowing he was the only one who could really understand, but he declined.

The call from the police had trumped what had been a traumatic breakup. After a few awkward adjustments to intimacy, finding ways to connect while not dating, we slowly found a more cautious comfort in our friendship. Now, on the river, for the first time, I missed having Peter next to me. This place was holy, and it was empty, and I stood on that gravel bar very much alone.

What did it mean when people said things like, "They are

always with us"? That we remember them? It was a platitude, tinny, the chatter of a child's toy meant to entertain. Where precisely was the "heavenly home"? I wanted GPS coordinates. I wanted a precise understanding.

And what I wanted was inconsequential. I understood that faith requires believing without seeing, accepting mystery, and that was fine as far as believing in God was concerned. But I didn't want mystery here. I wanted clarity.

The void opened in front of me again. Dad had been reading *Where the Sea Breaks Its Back*, an account of Alaska's first naturalist, Georg Steller. The bookmark and receipt were still tucked in the pages when it appeared in the box of personal effects left from Dad and Kathy's campsite. Dad had bought it at Title Wave Used Books in Anchorage four years before his trip. I can see him walking the aisles, perusing the shelves, picking up his copy, putting it under his arm, not quite getting to it, rediscovering it on his own bookshelf, packing it in a plastic bag for the trip. When he and Kathy called, I imagined them as I'd seen them in pictures of their trips — books at their sides, tea in their mugs, sitting in canvas camp chairs with the brick of a sat phone, facing the river, the perfect Arctic light on their faces, looking across with meditative satisfaction to the spot where I sat now.

I wonder what those mountains behind them might tell me, what advice they would give, if they could talk. What they would tell me about love, and about loss, and about how this wild place could heal as naturally as it could kill? But I was trying too hard. This kind of wisdom comes slowly, if it comes at all, and of its own accord.

Ned walked up behind me. I startled, but kept my gaze on the water.

"It's not okay," he said tersely, as though to the river. I kept a guard up, but his pain washed through me. I felt it like a shudder.

I was accustomed to his violence, and he to my sarcastic

comments holding him at a distance. The threat I felt from him constrained my compassion. One time this barrier had cracked temporarily. Years ago in the army, my phone had rung at a late hour. I was already in bed, and I rolled over to pick up the phone, squinting into the darkness of my bedroom to find the receiver. The sounds of a party popped and snapped. "Hello?" I said groggily. "Hello?" I don't know why I didn't hang up immediately. The undertone of a voice gurgled against the background of raucous laughs and yells. "Hello?"

I was about to hang up when I heard, "Shannon?" in a cracked, low voice.

"Hey." I woke up partly, shocked at the call, recognizing Ned's voice. He was studying for his PhD on the East Coast. I hadn't talked to him in months.

There was more crackling, gurgling. "I love you," he said, a quiet statement, almost like a sob.

I blinked into the blackness of my room. "I love you too," I said, letting each word out with care.

No response. Only the sounds of the party.

It was midnight. "Okay, I'm going to hang up now," I said into the receiver. I hung up and rolled over to my cat, who was curled up next to me under the covers. "What do you think that was about?" I asked her. She purred a little in her sleep, and I nestled in next to her, burying my fingers in the fur at her throat.

That had been many years ago. Our relationship never changed. I still regarded him with suspicion, maintaining a defensive posture against his abusiveness, interwoven with threads of persistent hope and tempered by sadness recognizing the fragility beneath his spiny surface. It was not that we were so different; it was that we were so much the same. I assumed he had likely grown past much of his anger, but enough indicators persisted that I still didn't feel safe around him. Dad would have liked it if we could have leaned on each other. But it wasn't up to Dad anymore. Maybe it never had been.

"No, it's not okay," I said slowly. "This trip won't make it okay. It's never going to be okay." I watched the late afternoon sun on the empty beach across the river. "It's not supposed to be okay."

We both stood looking across at the empty beach for what felt like a long time.

Requiem

Sanctus

Holy holy holy.

I look forward to Monday nights this first fall back from Alaska, after the funeral, after clearing out the house, anxious for the weekend to end and to begin the week and rehearsal. I keep my score on the piano in my small apartment, where I will be reminded with a glance: Mozart. It is assurance and challenge.

There are rehearsals that make me squirm, but most tap into an undefined place inside where body, heart, and soul come together, a place I can feel between my forehead and my stomach, a place I stroke by inhaling and exhaling, bringing in air, releasing it on melodies and harmonies deep and sweet, complex and beautiful.

This music that has been washing over me is beginning to sink in. I am starting to hear the melodies again, to appreciate the harmony, to hear the dissonances come and then resolve. I am beginning to learn beauty again.

Now, in late fall, most of our rehearsals include the whole choir, men and women in concert, singing the parts each group has been learning for the past several weeks. At first it is like holding a hand, this coming together, and then like a small rain shower, and then a gathering storm—the rain and the wind, clouds moving and darkening and the slick smell of water, and trickles and torrents. It is the storm abating, the clouds breaking, the first rays of light, the rainbow. It is pleading and angry, terrified and consoling, all of these different voices coming together and making this music that brings us out of ourselves, out of that rehearsal hall, out of the hard metal folding chairs looking across at I-5, into a force beyond any one or even all of us, into something terrible and beautiful and ultimately redemptive. Or this is what I hope. This is what I'm counting on.

CHAPTER 12

DESERT SPRINGS

Each light, each life, put out, lies down within us.
– Galway Kinnell, "When the Towers Fell"

Six weeks before departing for the Arctic, with the trip scheduled and gear in place, if not quite packed, I found myself landing in Phoenix after an urgent call from Aunt Marcia. Grandma
had collapsed, and despite beating the odds so many times in
previous years, this time she wasn't going to make it.

Speeding west on I-10 from the Phoenix airport to Sun City,
I grasped the steering wheel hard, squinting into a too-bright
day with a sickening sense of repetition. A phone call. Events
from far away, important events, with no warning and limitless
implications. In my selfish interpretation of what was happening,
I drove toward news of losing a key piece of my identity and my
foundation, a piece I'd leaned on more heavily in Dad's absence.
The tiny reserve of strength I had been collecting over the past
ten months drained away like water through a sieve. In the past,
I would have leaned on Dad for strength, even as I would have
wanted to be there for him in his pain. Now, even as I felt my
energies ebbing, I also felt a sense of responsibility, a sense that I
needed to be there especially because Dad could not be. I wanted
to be there for Grandma. I had to be there for Dad.

My knowledge of my grandma was limited to that of a grand-
daughter, but this let me spin her story as heroic. She'd been

an only child in Axtell, Kansas, a tiny town on the border with Nebraska. She had dark hair and flashing brown eyes. In high school she played basketball, and she eloped at sixteen with the boy she loved. Her father refused to speak to her for nearly a year, and she continued to live at home, keeping the marriage a secret from everyone outside of family so that she could finish high school, since students were not allowed to stay in school if they were married. My aunt Georgia was born two years later.

When Georgia was six months old, Grandma's husband was killed in a car accident. She was a widow at nineteen. In what she described as a heartrending decision, she left Georgia with her parents and went back to college at Kansas State, where she met my grandpa, a quarterback on the football team in the years of leather helmets. Grandpa had a quick smile, liked to play practical jokes, and went to church as often as she did. After they married, Dad was born, and then Dad's youngest sister, Marcia, and finally Tom.

In her twenties, Grandma learned to fly a small plane. I still can't understand how a woman from a tiny Midwestern town had either the idea or the guts to do this, but it makes me proud, and I like to claim a bit of that spunk. Shortly after she began her lessons, though, episodes of vertigo stopped her short of earning her license. Later, doctors found a benign brain tumor they opted to leave in place. She raised her family and supported her church in small Kansas towns with joyful Midwestern efficiency, bringing other families who were down on their luck into her home and running the youth group for years. Grandma's favorite thing was having family gathered around her dining room table, eating off her china at holidays or any occasion for celebration. She loved to decorate with pretty things — candles with sparkles and trains of gold-leaf ivy draped over a mantle or a shelf for Christmas.

She was not a beautiful woman. Her face had the plain bones

of a prairie woman, and she put on weight starting in her forties until she was quite heavy. Even so, she took time to dress well, every day, even without the means to spend much. She wore jewelry and bright colors and never went out without doing her hair and make-up. "I've always thought that taking a little bit of extra time to look nice helps brighten other people's day," she said. She never sent a card on time for birthdays or Christmas, but I never doubted her devotion. After Grandpa died, she went on mission trips around the world: Israel, Burma, Thailand, Russia. My dad was frustrated that she was spending the little retirement money she had to travel, but she needed a sense of purpose in her life. Whenever she talked of Grandpa, tears filled her eyes, even twenty years after he was gone.

Grandpa died when I was in junior high. We kids didn't get to go to that funeral, because my mother had custody that week, and she didn't allow it, something I had suspected only confirmed going through files after Dad died. This knowledge made me angry and happy, all at once. Years after Grandpa died, Dad came down to visit while I was attending Command and Staff School, the captain's staff course the army held at Fort Leavenworth. We spent the weekend together driving through the little towns in Kansas where he had grown up, first visiting Grandpa's grave in Topeka.

We pulled into the graveyard, stopping in front of the registry, running our eyes over rows of names engraved dully into polished stone until we found it: Ralph L. Huffman. We drove toward a tree in a corner of the cemetery.

"I think it's right around here," Dad said.

We got out of the white rental sedan and swung the doors shut. They swung too easily, slamming with a hard finality. I followed Dad down the manicured lawn past regularly spaced headstones set low to the ground. The thick smell of freshly cut grass hung heavy in the humid spring air. We both wore sunglasses.

Dad's long legs walked slowly, finally stopping in front of a shiny stone that read "Ralph L. Huffman." Dad crossed his arms over his chest. He looked down, his eyes hidden behind the dark lenses. Next to Grandpa's stone was Grandma's, with her birth date and a dash followed by an empty space. I focused on this as much as I did on Grandpa's grave. At the time it seemed to me morbid to have your headstone set before you died. I still thought death was something that happened to other people. It also seemed loving in a way I didn't yet understand, a love that meant you lived your life with another person, wholly, completely, until both of you were put underground.

Dad's six-foot-four frame rocked back and forth, almost imperceptibly, the way it sometimes did in church. I didn't know what to say. I stared at the stone. Shouldn't there be flowers growing around the grave? Modern graveyards don't have space for that. The shiny stone sat quietly. How could that tiny little line, that little dash between years, hold so much life in it, so many memories? That dash stored the big laugh Dad had inherited. That dash held memories of sitting on Grandpa's lap in his recliner, his magic tricks and goofy sense of humor, walks when Grandpa, with practiced sleight of hand, plucked lollipops and even ice-cream bars from trees. It must have meant so much more for Dad standing next to me behind his sunglasses, more in the way Dad's would for me someday, in the way all lives do for someone, somewhere, if we're lucky.

After that trip I wrote Dad a card. I found it in a box the summer he died. This is what I remembered writing: "Dad, I wish I had put my arms around you and hugged you when we stood by Grandpa's grave. I can only imagine how much you miss him, because I can't imagine ever losing you; it is my worst nightmare. I love you so much." But what was on the card was different: "Dad, it meant a lot to me to go with you to the towns where you grew up and to Grandpa's grave." So much left unsaid. Did he know what I wanted to say?

More than twenty years later, I arrived in Arizona when Dad could not. The wave of dry heat evaporated energies I hoped I might have. I drove directly to the hospice. Aunt Marcia met me in the lobby with the hurriedness of someone operating on the final wisps of hope. "You won't believe it!" she said. "She's awake and talking!"

We walked to the end of the quiet hallway to Grandma's small, clean room, where she lay in bed, a light blanket partly covering her, her head and shoulders elevated and her eyes closed. An acacia tree was just visible outside her window through the thin curtain and filtered the Arizona sunlight.

I walked up to her bed softly and stroked her hair back off her forehead. Her hair was still brown and coiffed as she took care to keep it. Dad loved it when we combed his hair when we were growing up. He'd have us walk on his back in the living room or comb his hair when he was reading on the couch. It was one of my favorite things too.

"Hi, Grandma," I whispered. She opened her soft brown eyes slowly, the same eyes Dad and Aunt Marcia had, the same eyes I have.

"Hi, honey," she said softly, with a smile dampened only by the exhaustion of letting go of life. Grandma looked so small in that bed, shrunk from her once formidable weight, but her eyes still shone.

"How are you doing?" I asked, smiling at her, feigning cheer and feeling false. I understood why it is said that hearts break. I'd understood for a while now. Underground rivers of sadness scald like fire. And so I felt that ripping and burning of a soul and a heart, breaking in relief at talking to her, breaking in seeing her face and holding her hand, breaking as I felt Dad and Kathy's absence and knowing they would want to be there too, breaking because I was losing her and I didn't know how much more loss I could bear. There should be a moratorium on deaths in our family, I thought, and winced at trying to make a joke.

I stood in the midst of that still water of all humanity, a pool that once accessed can never be forgotten, that says that everything will come to an end, everything will die, and that at the bottom of all of our lives is loss. It says love comes with loss, and life comes with death, and that there is pain unimaginable in this. At least that's what I thought it said then. I don't know what it is like to drown, to give in to liquid closing over one's head and filling one's lungs, but I imagine that at the end, there is a moment when each of us has to let this pool close over us, give up the desperate gasps for air, and reach for the depths where we believe another world awaits, or not.

"Oh, I'm doing okay," she said slowly, her eyes closing again, the tiniest of smiles flickering on the corners of her mouth. I held her hand, watched her shallow breath come and go, and then walked quietly out of the room. I walked to the end of the hall. I walked back to her room, looked in at her sleeping. I walked back down the hall. What was there to do? What could I do? My movements were as aimless as the desert tumbleweeds outside.

I tiptoed back into Grandma's room later in the day. Grandma's eyes opened slowly. "Honey, do you know how much I love you?" she asked, more quietly and slowly than normally.

"I know, Grandma," I said.

"You're always moving ... so fast ... all those places you go ... I worry about you so far away." Her voice was labored and quiet. "I love you so much. I just want you to know how much I love you."

Family continued to trickle in. Grandma grew stronger, and more and more lucid. A day into her time at hospice, she decided to resume her dialysis.

"Oh, I think I will," she said, with strength in her voice. Some laughed, and some cried, exhaustion, relief, frustration swirling into separate whirlwinds of grief for each person. The decision to continue dialysis meant she would have to leave hospice care. I did not know what to think. I did not want her to die. She was my last and closest link to Dad. What I wanted, though, had nothing to do with how the days unfolded.

After dialysis, Grandma collapsed again. Time warped: each moment sped by; each spanned an eternity. The concierge called an ambulance. We headed back to the hospital. Someone has said that suffering stretches the heart, so that after it heals, it can hold more love. But I felt as though my heart were stretched to the breaking point.

Back in the ER, Grandma began a series of X-rays and other tests. I walked beside her wheelchair to X-ray, holding her hand as the attendant wheeled her down stark white hospital halls. Every step took on the gravity of years — years gone by, and years yet to come without her. I trod unwillingly amid shifting verb tenses: she lives, she lived. The brain takes time to train in those tenses, and the heart must train to hold the weight of the change, all the while adjusting to an understanding that we are sinking deeper into the pool at the bottom of sadness.

"Grandma, what do you think about how to find the right person to spend the rest of my life with?" I asked, ignoring my awkwardness, feeling the window closing on her guidance and insight.

"Oh, honey," she said, with a small tired smile and a look into a close distance, as she did anytime she thought of Grandpa.

"Find someone steady. The rest of those things don't matter at all ... just find someone steady." I asked her about kids. "Love them, love them, love them," she said. "Now of course that doesn't mean be easy, but just love them!" I wished I could imprint her words in my mind, use them to bolster me for the rest of my life. I felt reality shifting and surging below me. I had not had enough time with her. I had not had enough time with Dad. I look back and understand I had not yet begun to grieve for Kathy. I had not had enough time with her either. What more should I ask? What wisdom of Grandma's would I need to survive the years ahead? What wisdom of Dad's, learned from Grandma, should I discover?

What mistakes did she make she could tell me to avoid? It was too late to ask Dad. It was too late to ask at all.

Minutes with Grandma rolled away like mercury. I walked back with her as she was wheeled back to her room, and paced in and out of the automatic sliding doors of the ER, out into the unforgiving burn of the sun, back into the cold sterility of the hospital. Neither offered any comfort.

The next morning, dark circles hung under Grandma's eyes, and she winced even propped against pillows. She had talked with her doctor before any of us arrived. She looked around at each of us slowly, resigned and determined and tired, all at once. "I've decided it's time to leave you," she said, her voice wavering just a little. "It makes me so sad." The clarity with which she expressed herself amazed me. "I hope you know how much I love you," she said to all of us, as she had to each of us individually.

She was choosing to leave life. How is it that we are called upon to make the greatest journey of our lives at the time of least strength? Her choice was inevitable, perhaps, but it was still a choice. Dad and Kathy had been stolen away. All of them waited for the ferry crossing that great river. As one day would I.

We sat with her for several hours before she was discharged. She asked for a comb so we could comb her hair — then, particular about the little wave that came down over her forehead, she insisted on doing it herself. She laid back on her pillow, eyes closing briefly. I wondered how she felt at the moment of decision, the moment of understanding. I don't imagine any of us can know that last shuddering release, the acceptance or the letting go, until the moment we arrive.

Back at Grandma's apartment, we helped her into her own bed to sleep, supporting her on pillows to keep her lungs free from fluid. The hospice nurse gave us instructions on the morphine Grandma could take for pain, as well as talking us through what we could expect. She warned us not to exhaust ourselves and suggested taking shifts each night and during the day.

While cousins came and went in the afternoon, I called Peter to talk, and then called another friend in Boston. They were short calls; I leaned into the cradling comfort of voices I knew loved me and were not a part of this play. My friend in Boston took just a few minutes to tell me a story: Her mother, a hospice worker, spent the first half of her life helping new mothers. She spent equal time bringing life into the world and helping life leave the world. In her mind, both represented births. In both cases, she helped a life begin. The weight of the day lifted just slightly, but not enough to quench my sense of dread.

Aunt Marcia and I took the first shift.

We laid mattresses on the floor of the apartment. I set my watch alarm for every half hour, finally lying down to sleep with the hallway light on. Grandma's breathing came raggedly, the sound of fluid overtaking her lungs. More horrible was when she woke, coughing and crying out. The resuscitation after her initial collapse had broken her ribs, and her coughing ripped through her body in waves. I jumped up each time to hold her hand, resetting my watch alarm to wake me up on the next half hour to give her morphine. Her wakings were far more frequent than my alarm, pain tearing her from sleep. After the first two episodes of her waking, I went in and curled up on the bed next to her, holding her hand. Although her eyes were closed, I felt her smooth skin over bony fingers squeeze my hand.

Still, every half hour or so she woke. The intensity of her coughing pushed her body off the pillows. Once, her body threatened to slide off the bed completely, her lace-trimmed white cotton nightgown riding up against old, soft skin, the nightgown of an old woman or of a little girl. I knelt over her, one knee on each side, supporting her under her arms, and moved her back on top of her pillows. Her body shook with deep and ragged coughs. With eyes wide open, as though she were looking not only at me but through me and through this life, she whispered my name once: "Shannon." It was almost a question.

"It's okay, Grandma," I said, and felt like I was lying, lying to this woman who was dying, this woman who was my father's mother. "It's going to be okay." I hoped that she couldn't hear the echoes from my rotting emptiness. I was alone on a shore trying to fight off ocean waves with a storm closing in. I smoothed her hair back from her cool skin.

There was nothing glamorous about this. But something else emerged about these waters of shared humanity: that pain too much to handle also comes with exquisite beauty, as common as dirt, as unexpected as grace. Are we meant to be pilgrims of the depths? It struck me that there is no greater intimacy than sitting with someone traversing that tenuous boundary between worlds, sitting vigil with a spirit trembling on the border, reaching toward the new and releasing the old. It seemed to me that our fragile humanity experiences this intersection only rarely because we are not strong enough to bear it more often, because what we live in those moments will take us a lifetime to begin to understand.

Resting next to Grandma in the semidarkness of her room, the hallway light leaking in through her door, I was poignantly aware that this was the thing I would never be able to do for Dad. And yet stroking her hair, I smoothed back Dad's hair. Staying with her in her pain, I was with Dad in his.

Grandma slept more soundly as the drugs took effect, and the cool night sizzled into the heat of another scorching day. In the afternoon, I drove to Aunt Georgia's house a mile away to take a nap. At 4:30 I bolted awake. A minute later my cell phone rang, and Sam urged me to come back to Grandma's apartment. I sped through the wide, sunbaked streets to her building and sprinted up the stairs. I think I knew already that she had left us.

Requiem aeternam. Grant them eternal rest.

CHAPTER 13

BARREN SANDS OF A DESOLATE CREEK

I am bound, I am bound, for a distant shore,
By a lonely isle, by a far Azore,
There it is, there it is, the treasure I seek,
On the barren sands of a desolate creek.

—Henry David Thoreau, *A Week on the Concord and Merrimack Rivers*

6/20/05
Camped at 69 degrees, 27.422' Elev 1364'
We planned a very early departure to help avoid the horrendous afternoon winds we've had. But at 4:00 AM there was pea soup fog to the ground so we slept till 6:00 and it had lifted a lot. By 7 it was a pretty day again. We packed after breakfast and set off at 10:00. The day progressively got more and more rapids. We stopped to scout many of them and all went well.... We stopped at 3:00 and both were tired ... but the wind never got real bad today—although it has never really stopped. The tent is up by 5:00 and it's getting cloudy. We both had a great day and tomorrow will pass the most difficult rapid and leave the mountains behind for the coastal plains. Rich

Wow! What a beautiful day on the river, challenging, somewhat stressful and full of surprises. We awoke at 4 AM but didn't get up until 7 because of fog.... We became aware rapidly that we were descending in elevation as we started to go through more challenging rapids especially as the river became one channel. After a few challenging ones I asked Rich and he concurred that we should start scouting before we ran, especially when rounding a bend up against a canyon wall.... We ate part of our lunch there and continued downriver, stopping frequently to scout. Rich ran two for me.... Tomorrow we'll finish the canyon run with the Class III rapids. Then we'll camp after we get through that and take a rest day.... We've lost all track of time and I'm not even thinking of "heading to the barn" like I was last year.... Life is simple. I should remember that.... PS very little horrendous wind today. It was tolerable for a change. Kathy

We slept hard that night after visiting the Father's Day Camp. We were still two days away from Dad and Kathy's final campsite. When we woke, it felt as if the sun had abandoned summer midstride. A freezing wind lashed at our faces. I hunched into my dry suit and PFD. The wind bullied our raft as we tried to maneuver around rocks and through rapids. We strained against the paddles, against the wind, trying to stay in the current.

Dad and Kathy's journal indicated a rough trip last year, constantly working against the wind, and a part of me was thankful for the shared experience. I was excited to come to the place they found so beautiful, to share their frustrations as well as their joys. But first we had to share the fighting of the wind.

"Come on, paddle hard!" someone yelled. The wind whipped against us and the raft ignored our struggles.

"Get it away from that rock!"

"I'm trying!"

All three of us paddled with all of our strength. The raft lurched, just skirting the rock, and then: "Left! Paddle hard!"

Our bodies were the paddles, pulling, begging.

"Dammit!" Sally yelled, and I saw her blue plastic paddle shooting downriver, even as her round body teetered over the side of the raft and toward the water. Clenching my paddle, I jumped up and over, grabbing her dry suit as Ned did the same. She rolled back into the boat, and the moment we knew she was in, we were back at our stations paddling.

"We've got another one. We've got to pull over!" I yelled, biting down hard as though my teeth might somehow steady our raft. "Paddle right!" Ned paddled from the bow and I put my body into it from the stern.

"Paddle hard! Back-paddle ... we're in!" The raft slid neatly into the eddy, and I was momentarily surprised that anything could pull us out of that terrible wind. I exhaled forcefully. "This is brutal!" The tension in my jaw became its own discomfort, building each moment.

"Yeah," Sally said. I waited for her to say more, but nothing came.

With quick, sharp movements, Ned began loosening the straps holding down the bags so we could access the spare paddle. I felt privately furious that Sally had made no admission of culpability, no apology, no guarantee of future caution, no discussion of the necessity of maintaining our gear in the wilderness. I was glad we had a spare. From this point forward, though, there was no reserve. And we hadn't even hit the canyon yet.

We wiggled the paddle out from its spot in the bottom of the raft and handed it to Sally.

"Well, it will be nice to get to Esetuk Creek," I said, trying to fill the gap in conversation. No one responded.

"Let's go," Ned said, and we pushed off from our resting place into the teeth of the wind.

Back in the river, as we fought the wind and the current through a succession of rock gardens, steep bluffs appeared on both sides and stark mountains rose behind them. Snow traced the ridges and cuts of the mountains like a crown.

Birds hung in the air, easily defying forces of air and gravity.

The Inuit look at birds as spirit, and I remember growing up seeing birds and animals as special. I read through the James Herriot
books quickly and jumped at the chance to volunteer at a local vet-
erinary clinic which specialized in wild birds. Once a week I took
the bus from school and helped with cleaning cages and holding
wiggly animals for exams, progressing to giving subcutaneous
shots.

The worst cages to clean were those of the wild birds. Occasionally a menacing bird of prey perched in the kennel at the end
of the row in the large dog area, contained by a plywood board
set over the kennel. The head veterinarian was the only one who
touched those birds, but they watched me with even and intent
eyes as I worked across from them. I had little doubt they would
rip out my throat given half a chance. I cleaned the cages of the
less threatening seagulls and ducks. Before working at the clinic,
I had liked seagulls, watching them from a distance ride the wind
and the sea in white drifts. My perspective changed working with
them in proximity. I fed them dog food moistened with water,
and either the cuisine or the accommodations must have caused
offense, because as soon as I delivered food to the clean cages, the
seagulls stepped in their bowls, defecated, flapped their wings, and
spread the mess onto every square inch of the kennels. I reeled
at the stink.

Ducks recoiled from me, backing into a corner and hissing,
and snapped at me with their rubbery beaks. I could see the fear
in their eyes, felt sorry that this wildness was caged. Growing up
with so many wild animals around us, I understood freedom to
be as vital as oxygen.

One weekend I brought home a nest of baby birds someone
had dropped off at the clinic. Well-meaning people often brought
nests to the clinic, not realizing that the mother bird was likely
only away from the nest gathering food. The chicks always died.
But we took them home anyway, feeding them a thin gruel of dog

food and water through a syringe. My nest of fuzzy gray chicks, all beak and fluff, didn't last the weekend.

Birds gave life to the boughs all around our house. Because our glass windows rose two stories, reflecting the birch and spruce forest, birds basking in the brightness of a summer day frequently flew into the windows and died.

One day, the thud of a bird against the sliding glass door startled me out of my immersion in a book. Outside, the feet of a tiny sparrow reached up at me, clutching at a life already gone.

Another similar bird perched on the bird feeder. I walked carefully over. The bird did not fly away. I put my hand up to it, slowly. Still it did not fly away. When I nestled my finger under its tail, it stumbled slightly and I felt the light clutch of its claws. I felt guilty; I knew touching wild animals could cause them harm. I put it gently back on the bird feeder, where it continued to sit, dazed. I picked up the warm body of its friend, walked it down to the woods just past our lawn, and gave it a burial from the Episcopal prayer book, marking its grave with a white granite rock flecked with black biotite and hornblende. When I walked back to the porch, the little bird on the feeder looked at me and flew away.

There was never any question in my mind that all creatures were part of a divine creation, and that all of us were here together to do the best we could. Understanding and honoring death was part of that effort. Perhaps that is the wisdom of a child. The world has a way of throwing us against that bright, hard reflection of life and knocking the simple vision of truth right out of us. If we are lucky, or careful, or daring, our lives are all about coming back to our senses. So the wild birds of the Hulahula, keeping their distance, dancing in the hard wind, looked, to me, wise and capable and free.

From the raft, I watched the landscape as the banks on both sides of the river steepened. On the west side of the river was

Kikiktak Mountain, what geologists call an anticline, a geologically young structure of folded earth and rock. Because of its newness, erosion had not yet done its work, and the ridge was susceptible to the deep cutting of the river. This cutting created the bluff on the east side of the river and the steep green embankments rising sharply on each side. Based on this terrain, I assumed we were close to Esetuk Creek, and the GPS concurred. We paddled for the point and pulled the raft into the eddy off the inside of the curve.

We were immediately upriver of Esetuk Creek, a frolicking and joyous dance of clear mountain water bursting through a small canyon down to the river. Making sure the boat was secure, I took the shotgun and hiked up the hillside, a perfect succession of green and flower-covered plateaus spilling into one another like the creek below, just as joyous in its traverse. The hanging gardens of Babylon made manifest in the Arctic.

I sat and identified flowers nestled into the plateaus, purple lousewort and white mountain avens. Perhaps we are only here to name. But I was here for more. I wanted to name, and be named. I wanted to be healed. I picked up an old Dall sheep horn, shed many years before, slowly falling apart, its curve still evident and perfect in simplicity. Layers peeled away like flakes of skin, thin pieces of paper, a message lost in time. Its beauty signified death and a reminder that blood spilled and stilled was a part of what lived, and the wilderness claimed the pain of that death in a way the world did not. By claiming the pain, it bore also the beauty, and that message was not lost.

The month after the ground was piled on top of Dad's and Kathy's coffins, I walked back up to the cemetery and ran into Shorty there, his pickup loaded with watering jugs he had brought for the flowers on the grave.

"Do you ever think you see him?" I asked. I knew I was reaching.

"Oh, sure, I talk to him on the river all the time," Shorty answered, unloading the water from his truck.

I raised my eyebrows. "Does he answer?"

"Sure, sure," Shorty said. "We talk."

I wanted to ask, What does he say? Does he remember me, on the other side of life, wherever he is now? But I restrained myself.

Shorty paused at the side of the grave. "The older I get, the more I understand that the line between the living and the dead isn't much of a line at all." I see now his gracious handling, in the midst of his own grief, of my questions reaching for a truth that cannot be attained, and my reaching too for a father who was gone and who, despite my repeated unconscious efforts with people and questions, could never be replaced.

Walking to the edge of one of the plateaus, I looked down into Esetuk Creek. It was as clear as the mountain air, defined only by the foam of its vivacious descent. The sound of the shallow creek didn't carry the depth of the river's song, but its playfulness imbued joy into the Arctic air.

Dad wrote:

We stopped for lunch at the prettiest spot near Esetuk Creek. The creek came from a steep canyon into the river right between two rapids. We hiked up on a knoll and could see it all — canyon walls, blue green rapids in both directions and Esetuk Creek.

Kathy had written:

The most beautiful part of the river so far, at least for me! It was the confluence of the HH and Esetuk Creek. We climbed a knoll and there was the cloudy turquoise creek bustling through white rounded stones into a pool of turquoise water that ended the rapids of the HH. The view upriver and down was spectacular and we remarked what a wonderful camping spot the knoll would be.

Ned made tea to go with our Clif Bars, almonds, and raisins. Lunch was short. The canyon waited for us. But I did not want to leave Esetuk Creek. I wanted to sit with the curve of the river holding happy memories from last year as though they might change the tenor of history, change the course of both trips, but the river wasn't stopping. Our job was to stay on the river.

A

Over the past year, I'd read a pile of books on death and grief and losing parents. Most of the books did nothing for me; my tendency to read for understanding wasn't working. Answers slipped away like mist.

Two were noteworthy. The first was *A Grace Disguised* by Jerry Sittser, who wrote about recovering from the traumatic deaths of his wife, mother, and child. I remember from that book the idea of a strong oak in a garden, struck down by lightning. Though the oak is dead, the gardener's job is to make the garden around the remains of the oak beautiful. The other book I immersed myself in was Leon Wieseltier's *Kaddish*, written by a man who found strength in learning about and practicing the Jewish ritual of saying Kaddish in synagogue after his father's death. Though Wieseltier was a nonpracticing Jew, for eleven months he said Kaddish three times a day at synagogue, drawing strength from community, from study, from this prescription of prayer. I was amazed at the words of the Kaddish, which never reference death or grief but rather exalt God. It turns out that the Kaddish is not a unique prayer for the dead at all, but is said at many points in any given service, with one recitation reserved for mourners, as though to recognize grief, while retraining minds and souls sunk in despair to a life of praise and hope, as though to revive the bereaved. I longed for a similar prescription, a revival, a ritual to lend structure and meaning to my grief and remind me that I was alive. I craved direction, rules, structure. Without the discipline, without the practice, everything I thought I was looked at death and felt the gaping chasm of human impotence.

The first Saturday back in Seattle after Dad and Kathy's funeral, I called the answering machine of a neighborhood Episcopal church. I wrote down the service time. I set my alarm clock. I woke on Sunday morning, dressed, and drove to the little stone church. I sat in back. While in Alaska, I'd gone to St. Mary's for church on Sundays, and every time, the tears let loose like flash floods in a desert, always around the Eucharist. Each time, the deluge surprised me into fright and relief.

As I sat in the hard pew toward the rear of the Seattle church, the words and patterns of the liturgy emerged in a new way, as though someone were running a magnifying glass over the pages of the *Book of Common Prayer.* Words I had seen and read and prayed so many times jumped out: "communion of saints," "have mercy on us." I walked up the aisle to the communion rail finally understanding. I was relieved, amazed, and bewildered. The communion of saints: the line between life and death isn't much of a line at all.

λ

As beautiful as Esetuk Creek was, I didn't feel the same delight Dad and Kathy had. Too much hung on this trip.

We pushed the raft from shore, felt it release from rock and sand, and moved forward into the river.

We were entering the canyon.

From the moment we left the shore, the water surged and sped around the bend where we had perched, diving toward the canyon wall on the other side.

"Paddle both, paddle left!" I yelled. The side of the blue rubber raft came within inches of the canyon wall when the force generated from our paddling pushed it back into the current. We sailed down and through a hole, and the raft popped exuberantly out the other side.

Then a rock: "Paddle right!" A furious slashing of paddles, partly in air, partly in water, as the force of the river bounced the raft forward. The river was alive. She strained and roared and sped. We were at her mercy.

The river was hard and fast beneath the raft, hard and fast and furious and angry and rushing and swirling and crashing and smashing, and we stayed in the raft only by will and gritted teeth and flexed quads and the grace of God. On either side, the canyon walls, undercut by the current, blurred by, unappreciated in our focus on the complexities of the raging current as we paddled and leaned and yelled and paddled, paddled, riding out the wave trains and diving through the holes, soaked by spray and waves, hands slippery on the plastic paddles, until finally the river relaxed just a little and we relaxed with her, and she widened out and the water was more shallow and we scraped on gravel bars. Now we could see the tundra on both sides, and the rocks in the current, and the willows growing, and the pink wild sweet pea and the white moss campion and the green coastal plain stretching out ahead and the mountains soaring behind us, and ahead of us the blue sky that, just beyond the horizon, we knew touched the dark polar seas just recently free of coastal ice.

"I lost it!"

Another paddle jetted away in the current. I wasn't sure whether to scream or to cry.

"Eddy on the left!" I yelled. Ned paddled forward, hacking at the water. I pulled hard, back-paddled, and we stopped to regroup.

"Well, we don't have another paddle," I said. I couldn't look at Sally.

"We're just going to have to get out and scout each rapid carefully," Ned said. "It's a big raft. It's going to be hard going with two paddles." None of us made eye contact.

"That other group is just behind us, isn't it?" Sally asked.

"They probably want to hang on to their own spares," I said shortly.

"I'm going to check out what's around the bend," Ned said.

I followed. Thick clouds of mosquitoes hung in the air. I waved them away from my face, feeling the physicality of the swarm with each swipe. Walking along the willows, I yelled, "Hey bear, hey bear, we're out here! Don't worry about a thing! Hey bear!"

Past the bend, we saw only a set of innocuous rock gardens.

"Looks like we want to stay left starting about there," I said, pointing at the tongue of river pouring through two boulders at the top.

"Yep."

"Hey, what's the deal with Sally?" I couldn't help myself. "I'd think someone coming on a trip like this would have a little better understanding of where we are. We aren't on a day trip where there's extra gear in the car."

"I know," he said.

"This trip is to honor Dad and Kathy. I'm mortified that she wants to ask someone else for a paddle. We should be able to make this trip ourselves. But I don't know if we can get down the river with just two."

"I agree."

"Okay, well, I'm not interested in being the one that does the asking," I said. I set my jaw and bit my lip.

We walked back to the boat, balancing on rocks and swatting mosquitoes.

"We'll ask Karen when we get farther downriver," Ned said. "We can pull over for dinner and wait till they float by."

"Sure!" Sally said cheerily.

"When you ask her, Sally," I said thinly, "make sure you acknowledge that we understand this is the wilderness — and that the ethic out here is to be self-sufficient, to take care of yourself. I think that's really important." I measured each word carefully and then released it slowly.

"Okay," Sally said. I still couldn't make eye contact with her.

Something inside of me cringed, believing this crisis reflective of my own failure to plan, my shortsightedness in agreeing to our small party, my foolishness in even having considered such a trip in the first place. I was worried as much about being up to the challenge as about being able to complete the trip, about being good enough to have undertaken such a journey. Dostoyevsky's words rang in my ears with excruciating clarity: "There is only one thing that I dread: not to be worthy of my sufferings."

"Let's get going." We jumped into the raft, and Ned and I paddled back into the current. It was hard work. By the time we'd bounced through the rock gardens and stopped to check the next rapid, Ned and I both were exhausted.

"I don't know if I can do this," he said. I was alarmed by his statement, though I was happy that the next section looked benign.

"Hang in there. We'll get through it," I said.

"No, this one looks tricky. I think we should line it." He spoke flatly.

"Really?" I looked at him hard. His face was set, impassive.

"Yeah. I don't know if I can do it with just two of us."

"Okay, let's line it," I said, aware of a current more dangerous than the river.

We attached the line to the raft and walked it through the rapids from the bank, stepping through willows, eyes on the water, eyes on the boat. My disappointment over not paddling this short piece of water paled next to the prickling sensation of danger, the pressing in of emotional and physical exhaustion. It is, or should be, the unspoken rule to go with the most conservative opinion in the wilderness. So our decision to line the boat had been the right one, but it had let in a glimpse of something untoward.

We had left the mountains. Now the river flowed through a series of plateaus with deep cuts. After a dinner stop and the gift of a paddle from Karen's group, we made our way down smooth water, looking for camp close to 8:00 p.m. We had been on the water for ten hours.

I watched the shoreline. I gazed across the plain on either side, still as watchful, still as worried. The raft glided downriver under the soft angle of the sun. And then, looking back at the mountains, my breath caught. The mountains sat solidly and with a great gentleness, the foothills draped like fabric over the land, exquisite fringes of willow on the riverbanks, wet rocks glistening in the midevening sun. Just here was pure abundance.

It was not the landscape that held me, though. I was transfixed by the light. It poured over me, filled the corners of the land. It was as eternal as time and as fleeting as days, as infinite as God and as finite as the eyes beholding it. I was immersed and filled up all at once. It lived, it had a being, that light. There was peace in it. There was gentleness and assurance. Its essence was music.

Requiem
Benedictus

> *Though I claw at empty air and feel*
> *nothing, no embrace,*
> *I have not plummeted.*
> —Denise Levertov, "Suspended"

Though the Mozart Requiem is commonly performed, I have never sung it before this performance. It is not the monumental aspect of the piece that intimidates me as much as my aching need to sing it, an ache approaching pain. And I do not want to just sing it; even if I'm only a member of a large choir, I want to sing it well, to sing it for my dad, and for Kathy. The Mass for the Dead, or Missa pro defunctis, has been set to music many times, though Mozart's setting is perhaps the best known. There is much conjecture about the composition of the Requiem, but most historians agree that it was an opportunity for Mozart to find a new direction and depth in his music. As he began working full time on the Requiem in October of 1791, Mozart had premonitions that he was composing the Requiem for his own death. Immersing himself with fervor into his work, he fell gravely ill, and he died in December, his Requiem unfinished. His colleague, Franz Xaver Sussmayr, had to finish it for him. Even the best among us die with unfinished business. Even the least among us, I hope, have someone who will try to finish it for them. That, at least, is how I understand it.

The primacy of the chorus in the Mozart Requiem gives us more time to rehearse with Maestro Perlman than we might have had with another work. He rolls into our first rehearsal in his wheelchair, and I am astounded. Hearing Perlman play in numerous recordings, I have been awed by his utter mastery of the music, the passion of his performance. I had not known he was disabled. That man who conveyed the depths of passion in his work had been struck with polio at age four. And yet the energy and vigor he brings into the room exceeds that of an athlete.

Rehearsals for me are another mountain ascent. I go in with my red water bottle, feeling the grains of fine Hulahula sand in my teeth and questioning my sanity at trying to connect with Dad and Kathy through music and sand from the river. The powerful harmonies nestle into my head and heart and voice, pull me again and again through Latin liturgy, straighten the paths of my grief, soothe the inflammation of my soul.

Music philosopher Peter Kivy admits failure in explaining the importance of music. But he sees the performance of music as a ritual of community, "the sense of cooperatively wresting order from chaos."[7] The performance of music "literally makes one able to hear what to others is inaudible."[8]

Maybe it is the communal nature of the performance of universal harmonies that I so yearn for. The sense of community in grief coming from all of humanity's worship of the divine. The connection to all of humankind in our shared belief that there is meaning, and that there is something more. This connection reminds me that I am alive. It is the reason I cannot sit at my piano alone, but need to stand and sing the Requiem, one of many voices singing, to access a sense of hope in myself I cannot otherwise express. Though I cannot find the quiet spaces of my heart to hear God, singing gives me a structure to reach for that connection to him, to feel I am one of many voices working together, inadequate alone but important as a part. The doing and the discipline have a place. They have a place when the quiet places elude us. They have a place in bringing us back to silence, to the symphony of the universe.

Dad's older sister, Aunt Georgia, comes to visit from Arizona the weekend of the concert, along with my cousins Jamie, Leslie, and Shelby. George and Joanne come over from Port Ludlow as well. I hope Dad and Kathy know somehow that all of us pray the Requiem in whatever way we can.

Perlman's direction combines the ferocity of a blizzard with the precision of a surgeon. The care he takes and the inspiration he brings to the performance pull me in like a vortex. There is a depth in him I have not experienced with other conductors. But his eyes also hold a deep kindness, a true love for the music, a love for those performing it with him. I follow him with all I have. I look to him as I looked to my father when I was a small child. I look to him as I look to God. I look to him for salvation. It is never good to put this much on a person, even on a master. We expect too much.

CHAPTER 14

DIES IRAE

Would that it were so easy to find
the sacred in the massacred.

— Stephen Cushman, "Dark Meat"

I woke to warm sun on the walls of the tent. Seemingly from
nowhere, the melody of "Sunrise, Sunset" from *Fiddler on the
Roof* moved through me as though it were playing outside my
tent. Dad had sung this song, among others from *Fiddler on the
Roof*, on our way up to the cabin as I was growing up. Sometimes
he mixed in the blues and spirituals too. I blinked at the clarity
of each note moving through me. *"Wasn't it yesterday ..."* A cool
breeze kept the heat of the day and the mosquitoes at bay. "Hi,
Dad," I whispered to the breeze.

Ned and Sally were making eggs, but I opted to stick with
my usual oatmeal and a mug of Market Spice tea. The weather
was easy and almost comforting. Ahead of us the coastal plain
descended out and away from the mountains toward the sea. I
marveled at their courage. I did not want to leave those mountains,
sitting behind us so solidly, peacefully. I looked back at them with
longing. Already they were shrinking behind the foothills.

I was starting to realize that the reason I had stepped into the
raft in the first place was less to find Dad and Kathy than it was
to face the beast — and not the bear on the tundra but the lashing

beast of grief within myself. Leaving the safety of the mountains, I was exposed. We were coming closer.

Dad and Kathy's journal stopped after they reached the spot we would visit today. The pages were blank. Their last entries recorded that they'd had clear cold weather, the kind that invigorates more than it chills. They had time to rest, to look at flowers, and to walk in the hills. A chance to talk to the guided group on the river. The rare visit of a wolf. Enjoyment of a good meal. They were on river time. Their rhythms were river rhythms. They were happy.

6/22/05 Last night I woke to go to the bathroom and discovered the tent encrusted with snow! The boats looked frozen white; I woke up Rich, who got up, too. Then we quickly dove back into our bags. Morning revealed fresh snow on the mountains, and quickly the snow on the ground melted. Warm sun blessed our breakfast and we went on a hike into the hills. Great views and it was actually warmer away from the river. Saw lupine, mtn heather, wooly lousewort, blackened? oxytrope and lapland rosebay. Came back, had lunch and took a great nap. . . . Saw the rafters tonight. They get out the 25th. They reported the strip was not dried out yet. Tonight there is a very cool, cool breeze but tolerable with headgear and the warm sunshine. It's looking like crystal clear weather tonight . . . probably cold, too.

6/22/05 Today is a rest day. At 1:00 AM we got up and it had snowed! By 6:30 there was snow all around but the sun came out and it was gone by 9:00. After breakfast we took a hike up a ridge for a couple of hours — actually 3 — then back for lunch. We burned trash and took a nap and worked on a faulty stove. Then it was hair-washing time. Then dinnertime. After dinner the two rafts we'd seen went past and we exchanged greetings — they appeared to be a guided group. Kathy's identifying flowers and

I just checked the maps. Our plan is to go 8 miles a day for the next couple of days and then call about the airstrip. If it's not dry we'll have to hoof it to the portage over to Opiklek Creek and then on to Arey Island for pickup. It's a beautiful evening with clear skies, but still a very cold north wind! Rich

6/23/05 69 degrees, 40'347 800' elevation. Awoke to beautiful blue skies. Warmest day so far. Left at 10:30 and continued down the river, still expecting the Class III rapids. We went through rapid after rapid, very challenging because of rocks everywhere. You rarely can take your eyes off the river or surely a rock will be right there!... At this point the mountains seem very far away. The rocks along shore are covered with vegetation resembling seaweed over rocks by the ocean. We saw a lone gray wolf while searching for a place to set up the tent. This camp is loaded with wildlife sign: bear and caribou tracks, moose droppings, ptarmigan feathers and droppings. I called my mother and we spoke briefly at $2 a min. Was good to hear her voice—she sounds happy. The sun is very warm and the wind isn't too strong. Still, I'm wearing everything to stay warm. This is an incredibly beautiful river and has been a challenging trip so far. Lord, thank you for our safety and guidance. Please continue to be with us in all that we do and say! Kathy

6/23/05 Woke to brilliant sunshine and blue sky—little or no wind. Left at 10:30 and spent the day picking through rock gardens. Rapids continue to base of river it seems! We went about 8–9 miles and stopped on a river bar for night. We saw a grey wolf! No 3 for the trip. Also saw a pair of rough legged hawks and assorted songbirds and ducks. The day stayed beautiful but wind picked up. We called our moms on the satellite phone. They were well. Beef stew for dinner—yum. We will try to look at our digital photos tonight in tent. Rich

We had passed the main rapids of the Hulahula, but today we had rapids of another sort to navigate. We didn't talk about it, except to confirm coordinates. An hour after breakfast, the sun had ascended and burned through the light breeze. I put my PFD on over my tank top, and sunscreen on my bare arms. We pushed off into the icy water. Another song flowed into my consciousness, mingling with the running river: "Deep river," the old Negro spiritual went, one of that canon of prayer known as sorrow songs, "my home is over Jordan. Deep river, Lord, I want to cross over into campground."

I was not sure what I was hoping to find, or what I thought might change. My growing sense of dread balanced against the understanding that this was someplace I had to be, something I had to do. The river's sonority offered a temporary comfort against the dissonance of growing chaos, the sounds of the biggest rapids ahead, rapids that had little — and everything — to do with a river.

The river was rolling and gentle now. The raft bounced easily through small wave trains, moving happily on the glacial water. I watched the tundra carefully. The bank rose to a low plateau on the left, obscuring what was beyond, and the plain rolled away to the horizon on the right.

Ned stared at the GPS. "I think it's right around here," he said flatly.

"No, this isn't it," I murmured. "It doesn't look like this. There should be a sandy beach." I almost hovered over the back of the raft, my legs flexed, leaning forward, watching the banks intently.

"That's it, on the right," I said, as the sandy shore came into view. My throat constricted. "Paddle both, paddle left!" I pulled back hard on my paddle, and the raft swung with a strange ease into the eddy. Beach met the bottom of the raft with a sound like sandpaper. Sally and Ned jumped out and pulled the boat onto the beach. Ned took the 45-70, put it over his shoulder, and strode wordlessly off into the tundra.

I walked slowly along the beach from end to end. The sand was unusual; other beaches along the river had been rocks and pebbles. I walked around the green tundra behind the willow copse beyond the beach. On the tundra, the low, tenacious plants of the Arctic crunched softly under my river boots. To the south, the hieratic heights of Michelson and Chamberlin stood in sacerdotal solemnity against a clear blue sky.

"Pretty out here, isn't it?" Sally asked.

I swallowed my disbelief. "Sally, I need some time by myself," I said.

"Sure, sure," she said, smiling.

There was something that bothered me those first weeks back in Seattle after the funeral. Something about needing information, even when it didn't serve any purpose. Information that couldn't be avoided and that came back to me now, on the beach.

It was the information about the bodies in the police report. They were just bodies then—not my dad, not Kathy. The bear had been eating them. And why not? He was a bear and had killed his prey.

Why had he started on Kathy? Perhaps Dad had died more quickly.

"Could he have had a heart attack?" a friend from high school had asked me at a coffee shop that summer.

"I guess so," I said, having no idea. It seemed likely to me that the coroner would not have conducted an extensive autopsy. Why bother figuring out if anything had happened aside from the attack?

In the last picture of Kathy, she is wearing a hat and a fleece coat. Behind her is visible the sand of the beach, part of her red inflatable kayak, a rock securing a corner of their tent on the sand. She smiles broadly in spite of the cold. The willow copse had shielded Dad and Kathy from the freezing northeast wind that day. Then it had hidden their bodies when the bear dragged them there—dragged the bodies, that is.

The picture in the paper showed the brown humped hulk of the grizzly at the north end of the beach, glowering at the photographers; the collapsed tent had been pulled to the south. I looked around the willow copse and the south end of the beach for evidence of a bear digging, for animal tracks. Dessicated indentations of caribou hoofs and one large wolf track wrote a story of visits from the previous year. Bordering the beach were yellow daisies, the blooms of Eskimo potato, but nothing more auspicious. On the beach itself, the sand lay firm and untouched, a slate washed clean, healed by water and wind.

In a story about the opposite end of the earth, Jorge Luis Borges notes that the landscape "is on the verge of saying something. It never says it, or perhaps it says it infinitely, or perhaps we do not understand it, or perhaps we understand it and it is as untranslatable as music."

The story that this landscape held, I knew in pieces.

Part of what I knew came from Jim. He was the last person to talk to Dad and Kathy. Jim and his wife, Carol, are owners and guides of Arctic Treks, one of the oldest Arctic river rafting companies. On June 23, 2005, he and an assistant guide, Cin, were rafting the Hulahula with three couples from Washington state. They had been on the river for a week. The water was running low, colder than normal temperatures slowing the typical freeze-melt cycle. It flowed thinly over gravel bars, a perfect blue, not muddied by the gray of upriver glaciers. But the raft was heavy, and the group had to get out frequently to pull it over gravel bars. Still, the eight rafters felt a sense of magic in the air and in the splendor of the Arctic landscape.

There were few other people on the river so early in the summer. The group had seen only two other people, traveling together in inflatable kayaks. Because the wind whipped most strongly in the late morning and early afternoon, the rafting group started late that day to miss the winds and ended their day late as well.

It really didn't matter, because the sun never sets. It's called Arctic time, this quiet shifting of schedules. There is light for your journey any time of day or night. This endless daylight lends a sense of well-being, a blissful detachment concealing the dangers of wilderness.

The couple in the inflatable kayaks were on the opposite schedule. They rose early in the morning to get on the river, stopping to camp before the winds picked up. Jim's group and the couple leapfrogged each other down the river through the Romanzof Mountains and the foothills leading out to the coastal plain. The rafting group noticed an impeccably kept camp, boots lined up neatly outside of the tent, boats pulled up well clear of the water. The night of June 23rd, when Jim's rafting group passed the kayakers' camp, the couple had not yet retired. They sat at their tent, preparing for bed. A cold northeast wind blew, but the couple had pitched their tent below a small bluff and a copse of willows to their east to shelter them from the elements. The man noticed the rafts coming and walked down to the shore.

The man and the rafters exchanged a few words of greeting. "There was something special about that night," one of the rafters later recalled. "There was magic, love in the air. Both of their faces shone with happiness — they loved being out there with each other. When we got into camp, we talked all night about what a special night it was, and how the couple we passed just radiated joy." Each of the couples recounting the story does so with tears glistening in their eyes, betrayed by that magic of Arctic light.

Like most stories, this one started even earlier than that. In the fall of 1997, I returned from Bosnia. I had led my second flight platoon, and we had flown the valleys of Multi-National Division North from our camp in Tuzla West in support of the Dayton Peace Accords.

As I was coming home from Bosnia, looking forward to going

home, somewhere in the Arctic the Inupiat caught their September whales. Millions of migratory birds set out toward southern climes, and silence settled over the tundra. Somewhere in that wilderness, a sow grizzly, impregnated in the spring by a male and well fed by the summer's bounty, wandered to the south slope of a mountain and used her long claws to excavate a den. She crawled in, escaping the swirling snow and icy wind and scarce nutrition outside. Her heart rate dropped to a few beats a minute. She slept. During that sleep, one or two cubs were born, tiny, hairless, and blind. The sow licked the mucus from their bodies, licked them alive, and they suckled in the new womb of the den.

One spring day in 1998, the sow brought her cubs out onto the tundra. One of these cubs — or maybe he was the only cub — will one day kill my dad and Kathy. He has never seen a human, but he will taste human flesh, only a day or maybe two before he tastes his own blood as he stumbles and falls for the last time.

It is possible that Dad and Kathy slept in their last day. It was cold outside, and they were tired. They were not in a hurry. The next day was their sixteenth anniversary. Each had brought a card for the other, protected in Ziploc bags.

Dad and Kathy were in the wilderness. They had always loved the wilderness, and with kids gone, they could take the time to enjoy it together. For all who escape to true wilderness, one of the reasons to go is that there is not another soul anywhere around you. You go to be engulfed in and connected to the majesty of creation. You go to forget yourself. There is no unnatural noise, no kids yelling, tires screeching, bosses nagging. There is also no one to hear you scream.

The yellow nylon of the tent flapped in the wind curling over the tundra bluff and copse of willows on the eastern banks of the Hulahula River. The flapping of a nylon tent can lull you to sleep, or in harsher winds keep you up all night. The continuous *snap! snap! snap!* of nylon and metal grommets can make you crazy.

Sometime in the morning, Dad, with pepper-and-salt hair disheveled from his week in the wild, sat up in his sleeping bag and unzipped the tent while Kathy remained in her bag. Maybe he got up to go to the bathroom, or maybe he had heard something. The tent zipper opened the cocoon of a tent onto a sandy beach and turquoise river water, just upstream from a small rapid.

The man drowsily unzipping his tent does not see just the river. The massive bulk of a grizzly fills his view. His heart jumps; his blood pressure skyrockets.

Gerald May describes the first time a bear comes into his campsite: "The bear is right next to me, its side brushing the tent canvas, its growl deep, resonant, slow.... It's like some kind of fierce embrace ... another deeper voice ... whispering 'Be frightened. Just be frightened.' ... My heart is beating so loudly I'm sure the bear must hear it. And I have never felt so alive."[9]

John Haines imagines an encounter with a bear: "The bear suddenly lunged from its hiding place with a terrible, bubbling roar and struck me down. In that instant of confusion and shock I was joined to the hot blood and rank fur at last. All my boyhood dreams of life in the woods, of courage and adventure, had come to the final and terrifying intimacy."[10]

And Mary Oliver's words:

... But not one of them told
what happened next — I mean, before whatever happens —

how the distances light up, how the clouds
are the most lovely shapes you have ever seen, how

the wild flowers at your feet begin distilling a fragrance
different, and sweeter than any you ever stood upon before — how
every leaf on the whole mountain is aflutter.[11]

Later I talked to a Gwich'in elder, Hannah Alexie. What did her people think when someone is killed, I wanted to know.

"An animal can get scared and need to protect itself," she said. "It just happens sometimes."

I wanted an answer. What did she think, two people in a tent, killed by *shih*?

"Maybe that animal was hungry," Hannah said. "Maybe it saw a tent, and it didn't know there were people. This can happen."

Maybe.

Did Dad see the sparkle of the river in slow motion, each drop of water moving past in slow seconds, trembling drop by trembling drop, against the calligraphic line of the opposite bank? Did he smell Galway Kinnell's "chilly, enduring odor of the bear"?

Dad reaches back to grab the rifle. He actions the lever. The huge beast collapses the tent with a swipe of its powerful foreleg and razorlike claws — or maybe Dad is alerted by the sound of unexpected commotion. He unzips the tent, to clear his shot at the bear and to facilitate their escape. But three hundred pounds of force behind that daggered paw swipes across his head, and whether his heart fails or it is the swipe of the bear, it is over. Kathy's screams divert the bear, and in less than a minute, the bear is the only actor in that space. The yellow cocoon of the tent becomes a shroud.

"A rupture of the earth," says the poet. This thing has happened, and nobody in the world knows. The distances light up. Ferocious intimacy. Final intimacy. Stolen intimacy. Intimacy forever lost.

In one of my many calls with Officer Holschen, he explained that a grizzly kills its prey by delivering a fatal blow to the head, strong enough that in some cases it decapitates its prey. Then it bites the neck, securing its kill. "Nineteen seconds," Kathy had told me, several months after she died, as I slept. "It lasted only nineteen seconds."

The bear ripped through the rest of the camp. Long claws engineered for digging for ground squirrels and tearing flesh collapsed the inflatable boats. Teeth and claws shredded gear. Food in bear canisters stored away from the sleeping area was left untouched. Powerful jaws and sharp teeth dragged Dad's and Kathy's bodies off toward the tundra, as bears do with their prey, to partially bury them as they were consumed.

I don't know what this was like. I don't know the terror, the sounds, the smells, the screams. Here is what Beryl Markham says about being attacked by a lion: "What I remember most clearly of the moments that followed are ... a scream that was barely a whisper, a blow that struck me to the ground.... I closed my eyes and tried not to be. It was not so much the pain as it was the sound. The sound of [the] roar in my ears will only be duplicated, I think, when the doors of hell slip their wobbly hinges ... it was an immense roar that encompassed the world and dissolved me in it."[12]

That is the best I can surmise. A roar that swallows the world and two lives.

A

Part of what I knew came from the newspapers. In the story relayed by the *Los Angeles Times*, many hours later, Robert Thompson, an Inupiat guide from Kaktovik guiding professor Kalin Grigg and his wife, Jennifer Stark, from Colorado, rounded a bend in the river and saw a grizzly on the north end of a sandy beach, pacing.

"Wow, look at that!" The clients were excited. Their cameras clicked away.

But as they neared the bear, Robert noticed the remains of a camp strewn across the beach. He hoped that whoever belonged to this camp was out hiking, but he had a sick feeling in his stomach. He pulled their raft over on the opposite side of the river. Robert pulled out the sat phone and called Walt Audi at Waldo Arms.

"Walt," he said, "this looks like a bad situation. We have a bear in camp with what looks like three smashed-up tents and we can't see anybody. We don't know where the people are. I think it would be a good idea if you got Search and Rescue up here quick."

Concerned about the grizzly, the rafters put back into the water to head downstream. Passing the beach, they watched the bear in the copse of willows behind the camp. Then, strangely, the bear lumbered down to the bank of the river and crossed it. When it disappeared behind a small knoll, they pulled over to observe. Kalin tried to keep his eyes on the area where the bear had disappeared. Robert was worried. For a bear to follow a raft was highly unusual. By now the rafters understood that there was cause for concern.

Kalin jumped up onto a boulder to watch the bear through binoculars. It rolled in the snow, appearing to play. It moved inland, and then came back toward the river, crabbing back and forth as though it were stalking. Jennifer pulled the raft back into the river and held it in the current. Robert yelled, "Let's get out of here!" The three jumped into the raft.

"Keep it in the current!" Robert yelled. He cocked his pistol, fully expecting to use it. He watched the bear. Kalin and Jennifer strained at the oars.

The grizzly followed them into the river, swimming toward them, then crossed the river and ran up the opposite bank. He charged downstream, almost next to the raft. The main current followed the bank exactly, and the bear was positioned perfectly to jump into the raft when it got close enough.

"Keep it away from the bank!" Robert shouted.

"But that's where the current is!" Jennifer cried.

Robert had never seen a bear do anything like this.

The bear dropped into the river just behind the raft. They could hear its paws slapping the water. Robert aimed his revolver at the bear, ready to shoot. The bear began closing on them, to within twenty feet.

Fortunately, Kalin and Jennifer were experienced in running rivers. Jennifer noticed a sleeper in the river, a large rock just below the surface of the water. "Let's shave it!" she yelled. "Paddle, now! Now!" They strained to paddle close to the side of the boulder, just skimming it. Moments later, the bear thudded against the rock. It scrambled to claw itself out of the water, and then stood on the rock, watching them pull away, water coursing off its brown fur, glistening in the sun.

Forty-five minutes later, Robert pulled the raft over and made a call to Walt Audi, giving the coordinates of the camp. "Walt, this is really serious. You've got to get somebody up there," he said. Walt called Barrow Search and Rescue.

Late that evening, close to midnight, a Bell 412 search and rescue helicopter navigated the ubiquitous coastal fog of the Arctic all the way from Barrow along Alaska's northern coast to the coordinates Walt had given. The pilots were Randy Crosby and Robert Mercier. Arriving at the coordinates, the pilots saw the gear ripped and strewn across the beach, the bear, and what appeared to be two bodies. It was not a rescue mission; it was recovery. They needed to fly back to Kaktovik to get the police.

The helicopter arrived slowly back in Kaktovik and landed in dense fog. Some Inuit believe that malicious spirits appear only in fog and darkness, angry about a taboo that has been broken. One pilot stepped slowly out of the helicopter, his face a mask of sorrow, shock, and horror. His voice was low, almost inaudible. This is what I had seen on the videotape.

The recovery effort was turned over to the police. Officer Holschen was approaching the end of his assignment in the Arctic. He and his wife and four children had loved their time with the people of Kaktovik, even adopting an Inupiat child into their family. Holschen was the officer who had to deal with bear problems in the tiny village, chasing away the polar bears that came into the village, and brown and black bears as well. And yet in his years of doing this, he had never had to kill a bear.

He needed help for this recovery, but help is in short supply in a tiny village off the northern edge of the continent. He asked two

German photographers to join him. The helicopter pilots waited for the fog to lift, then headed back out across the coastal plain.

At the campsite, the helicopter flared and landed, and the bear, startled by the rotors, ran off. But as the team worked at recovering the bodies, one pilot noticed the bear crabbing back toward the beach. Wild animals are frightened by the loud sounds and smells of a helicopter and usually leave the scene when a helicopter approaches. They rarely return.

The pilots took off again, flying toward the bear. With his shotgun and a few slugs, one pilot dropped the bear on the tundra. Now all of the actors on the scene were involved in recovery; the bear's carcass would need to be recovered as well.

Holschen called the Anchorage Police Department to notify the Huffman household. It was a Sunday morning. The Anchorage police rang the bell at our home off quiet Grover Drive on the Hillside in Anchorage, but the house stood silent. As the police walked down the driveway, they saw a neighbor out for a walk and inquired about Dad. It happened that the neighbor knew one of Dad's law partners, and the police called Don. Don came into the office late Sunday morning. He had worked with Dad for more than twenty-five years. I knew him to be mild mannered, bright, and kind. Instead of wilderness trips, he and his wife preferred golf. He didn't know where family phone numbers were, although he knew the general locations of us kids and that Dad sometimes paid his bills in the office. He found Dad's cell phone bills in the safe and gave the most frequently called Seattle number to the police. They called me.

Λ

I walked back to the beach. My boots sank and slipped in the sand. The river sang softly behind me. I knelt in the soft, gritty sand; warm tears stung my face. I recited the Lord's Prayer and the Twenty-Third Psalm. I'd forgotten my prayer book, and yet somehow the words of the Eucharistic liturgy flowed out of me. "On the last day ..."

The last day. My prayers, halting before, came easily. On this beach, I knelt with the Good Friday God, the suffering God who had wept and bled, cried out and died. The Easter God — that was who I'd been trying to talk to, but I wasn't ready. It wasn't time. First I had to pray to the Good Friday God, the one who suffered, before I could understand any part of resurrection. This was the gift of my faith.

"We believe," our priest had said, "that when we come together at communion, it is the indwelling of God, the communion of saints." The Reverend John Polkinghorne, both physicist and priest, says of the sacraments that they are "inklings of God's new creation, the redemption of the world beyond its death."

My hands shook; they felt hot in the sun. I opened the plastic bag I had carried with me from Seattle. In it were small wafers, blessed by my priest. My tongue was dry, and the wafers stuck to my tongue and the roof of my mouth. I opened the small plastic water bottle I'd brought with the bag. The wine was syrupy and warm. I felt it roll over my tongue thickly, then down my throat. In the heat of the sun came the inkling of indwelling, of communion not bound by matters as small as breath.

I stood up slowly and paced the middle of the beach, where Dad and Kathy had likely pitched their tent. The river had risen and fallen again since their trip. The sand was firm at the far edge by the willows. A cataclysm cleansed. The earth moved. The waters came. My eye was drawn, then, to a rock partly buried in the sand, out of place on the sandy beach. I looked around and saw another, and another. Five rocks, evenly spaced like the points of a pentagram, all partly buried. This was where their tent had been. They had used rocks to secure the corners on the sand. This was the place they'd died. Violence had been done here. Life had been lost here. This was the place where, even before I knew it, I had lost them forever.

The wilderness ethic is to leave no trace of one's travel. But it seemed that there should be something to mark this sacred place, this thin place. This place out of time — a sandy beach and an icy river and sun beating down. I picked up each of the rocks in the pentagram, sand wedging under my fingernails, and carried them to a spot above the high-water line, just under the willows. There were no other rocks on the beach, so I waded into the water and pulled rocks from the bottom of the river, feeling the weight of them in my arms and shoulders and back, the sense of release as they came loose from the sediment. The icy water cooled me through my dry suit, but sweat ran down my back from the sun. I staggered out of the water with each rock, walking it to the small pile at the base of the willows, the thud of it on the sand and on the other rocks both relief and pain.

Finally I had rocks enough for a small cairn. I looked at it, unsatisfied. This beach was where they had "crossed over into campground." I found two small pieces of driftwood and secured them in the shape of a cross with a piece of twine. Then I laid the tiny amulet of Our Lady of Guadalupe, blessed by Father Jack in Healy, in the rocks, letting it slip down into the dark spaces between them. I stepped back, slowly, and the energy drained from my body. "I love you," I whispered to the cairn. I listened, and watched, and heard only the wind.

Ned and Sally waited in the raft with snacks. I climbed back in, and as the raft moved smoothly into the river, I looked back at the beach. The river was gentle here, her murmurs soft. Ned and Sally paddled slowly forward, looking ahead. I looked back again, and again. And then the river curved and the beach was out of sight. I strained to see around the corner. But the river continued on. I looked ahead at the river before me.

Requiem
Lacrymosa

Dying, each sings at the edge of what he knows.
—Li-Young Lee, "Lake Effect"

S t. Augustine said that singing manifests itself not only as song but as love for him for whom we sing, a statement which has later been abbreviated as "he who sings prays twice." At times, I have not had words to pray. I believe that it is at those times that God prays for us. When we cannot sing, the universe itself sings. Physics prescribes it: As sound is produced, whether by bow over string, air over vocal cords, or breath through a wind instrument, it travels in a wave. Concurrently, that wave divides itself in half, in thirds, in fourths, *ad infinitum.* The sound itself both travels and divides, allowing us to hear overtones sometimes harmonic, and sometimes inharmonious, depending on whether the sound is an integer of the original sound produced. We hear one tone when another is played. In a very real sense, in silence plays a symphony we cannot always hear.

The night of the performance falls as quickly as winter in the Arctic. I stand in my designated row on the risers behind the orchestra on stage, blinking against the bright lights and concentrating on not locking my knees. I work to imagine Dad walking in the doors at the rear of the dark concert hall, coming in to take his seat, looking up to find me on the risers. But the doors remain closed.

Perlman comes out from behind the curtains stage right. His legs splay and his crutches angle out supporting his body. I wince at the juxtaposition of the elegant concert hall, the precision and poise of each instrumentalist and vocalist standing at the ready, and Perlman's halting ambulation. Yet as soon as he takes his seat to conduct us, the moment he sits down, Perlman is utterly in control of the orchestra and the choir, each of us mere instruments on which the music is played, demanding that our spirits and souls tune the strings and become music. The tension is resolved. His body has failed him, but the music will not. The connection to the spirit of life will not. I follow the baton as though transfixed. My gaze moves between my score, following where the black notes lead, and the wand Perlman wields. I tumble down the rabbit hole, no longer one but many, no longer earthbound but part of music soaring beyond the physical into all that is wild and real and deep and sacred. I am part of the music as a drop of water is part of a river, feeling the currents and eddies and flow, the crashing and tumbling and streaming, the whispering and sighing and moaning and rumbling. On wings of air and water and fire and earth, instruments, voices, and maestro fly in one great surge of prayer and harmony.

At the end of the performance, Perlman drops his arms. He smiles at us, broadly. There is applause. A standing ovation. And then we file off the stage, moving as one unit. The orchestra disperses too and once backstage puts away their instruments in black cases with pictures of family members taped inside. I walk back to the bathroom to pull off my polyester black dress and tights, to change into something comfortable for the drive home.

I am curiously not happy, not unhappy, but I had expected more. I had wanted salvific forces to surround me, the heavens to soothe my wounds, and they did not. But I have internalized beauty. I have internalized prayer. I have learned how to hear again. The dull ache that was there before the performance, that was temporarily lifted by breath and voice and absorption in the maestro and the music, settles back in, comfortably arranging itself in the void inside of me. If it is a little lighter, it is imperceptibly so. I can pray, it seems, and even sing, but I will have to wait. I will have to sit with this thing that weighs on me like a stone. I will have to work to will each breath for as long as it takes, though it feel like eternity. In this waiting, there is beauty, if I am willing to hear it. In this waiting, there is witness. But it is hard. I am not in control.

After singing Mozart's Requiem, I understand at once, an awareness coming like a gust of wind through a door, that my thoughts about going to the Arctic are not merely an interest but a necessity. I have to see the place Dad and Kathy loved so much. I have to see the place where they died. They had taken to rivers later in life, a departure from previous adventures. The river was their Requiem. I have to finish their trip.

CHAPTER 15

SLANTS OF LIGHT

Looking out of the window,
one of us witnessed what kept vanishing,
while the other watched what continuously emerged.

—Li-Young Lee, "Descended from Dreamers"

O ur campsite that night was a large gravel island bordered by green willow and covered in wild sweet pea. We set up the kitchen at the far end of a gravel spit and found a place inland for the tents. After dinner I excused myself for a bath. Carrying a bar of soap and a camp towel, I walked to a tiny beach at the other end of the island that was surrounded by willows but still allowed good visibility of the bank across the river and the island behind me. The constant vigilance weighted me down like lead; I also felt very much alive.

I was no longer surprised that the Arctic evening greeted me with disparate perspectives: the low light on the water, gentle as a touch, danced over the surface, inviting me even as I winced in anticipation of the glacial chill. As I pulled off my clothes, the cold washed over me the moment my skin was released from its encumbrances, from polypropylene weighted by odor as much as by fabric. First a jacket, then a long-sleeved polypro shirt, my camisole, my sports bra, my long johns. I stood naked on the small patch of mud, toes curling like a child's. My vulnerability—my sheer ineptitude, my lack of defenses in this wild place—shone in the whiteness of my goose-pimpled skin in the late night light.

The river lapped, frigid but tender, at my feet. I reached down and splashed the glacial melt up over my shoulders, pulled it up my arms, over my stomach, down legs bumpy with cold. My feet felt numb quickly; the rest of my skin, after the first sting of the water, merely cool. Though the soap barely sudsed, I rubbed the smooth bar over my body, caressed by water and pacific night air. Rivulets of river ran over my skin. I cupped water in my hands, soaking my hair. I rubbed soap between my palms and massaged my scalp, grimacing at the cold stabbing at my forehead. Slowly the shock of the water eased, and the water renewed me with its vigor.

I watched the water. I listened to the water. In it, I heard the sounds of rocks, low sounds of gurgles and streams and trickles. And I heard voices. Somewhere under the water, even in this shallow place, voices came out of and through the water. I could not understand them, but they talked back and forth with excitement and joy. I stopped still to listen; what I was hearing was impossible. But the voices continued. I wondered if they were voices of ancient peoples in this same place, if they were voices of another world, if I should be wondering at all, or only humbly reverent. I did not think it was Dad and Kathy; it was many voices. I listened with what I still believe was sanity. And I have come to believe that whatever it was I was hearing, whomever it was, I am meant only to know that there are worlds beyond my knowing, and that the only appropriate response is awe.

I stepped out of the water. A new layer of polypro, top and bottom, still clean, saved for this moment. A new pair of socks. I brushed through my snarled hair until it was smooth. Slowly, my body warmed to the new layers. The numinous quality of light warmed me all the more. The breeze kept mosquitoes at bay but did not chill. I sat on the bank, anointed by light pouring over the tundra, washing over me.

⋏

The next morning we had a quiet breakfast. No one spoke. I walked with my bowl of oatmeal to the shore and looked across the river, across the tundra stretching away on the other side. The sky labored under a muted overcast, and the light flattened out to something ordinary, less than ordinary, not worthy of the space we traveled. As we loaded the boats, Ned stood back, distracted, facing away and pacing. I noticed this, but stayed focused on the boat.

"Sally, want to grab that strap over there?" I asked. She stood on the other side of the raft. "Right, that one. See if you can tighten it down over those dry bags." Sally grabbed the strap and pulled it through the teeth of the buckle. We repeated the process with each strap holding the gear. "Well, it's not pretty, but I think it will hold!" I forced a note of cheer into my voice. "Ready, Ned? Think we got it all set." Without a word, he walked to the raft, and we all pulled it into the current. The water took us away.

I should have seen it coming. The biggest beasts on our trip still stalked us. I hadn't been paying attention. I'd thought the worst was over. I had faced the beach. I had made a monument. I had said my prayers. But I'd been selfish. I'd thought the trip was only about my own grief, my own issues, but unacknowledged grief is insidious, a shape-shifter, a poison.

The river braided mercilessly. Interrupted by frequent walking of the raft over riffles as the dispersed current barely trickled over gravel bars, unsure of the distance yet to travel, we resolved to make it as far as we could.

In these silent moments, the birds were our companions. A jaeger flapped its wings and soared, paused, dipped as its velocity lost to gravity, flapped its wings again. I hummed softly to myself. "Sunrise, sunset ..." slowly moving the steering paddle behind me. It gave me something to hold onto, this music and this wild.

And then it came out of nowhere, as suddenly as if a rip appeared in the universe around me. Ned said violently, "Shut up!"

I watched the river in front of me with eyes narrowed, searching for what lay beneath. It was a steady current. We rode it smoothly. I moved the paddle to keep us in the current. Sally kept looking forward. I clenched my teeth against whatever was happening, and hummed quietly, as a source of the only known in the present, the only thing I understood.

"Shut up!" he yelled.

I stared at the river. I did not look for answers or for help but tried only to stay in the current.

"You can't paddle this boat!" he yelled. "We'd be better off without you!"

I did not respond, and continued to hum softly, focusing on the breath it followed, looking to it for strength.

He continued to shout. I sat in the stern, relying on the pressure of the paddle against the water for stability. His words carried without his turning around, words that I had never heard directed at me before, words that did not bear repeating, names that were ugly and profane and laden with hate and pain.

"Why don't we pull over?" said Sally.

"That's probably a good idea," I said. We maneuvered onto a large, flat gravel bar in the middle of the river.

"Want me to stick around?" Sally asked, looking at me.

I smiled thinly at her and shook my head, just barely. She looked at me quickly and then said in a low voice only I could hear, "You know, there are some things that can't be fixed." Then she walked off twenty yards.

Ned got out of the boat. I was aware of the placement of the two weapons. I was also aware there wasn't anyone around for miles. Karen's group would already be back in Kaktovik.

A sneer warped Ned's face. I sat on the back of the raft. He walked over to stand inches from me, leaning down from his six-foot height and spitting as he talked. "You always have to be the one, don't you?" he said. I sat still and quiet, feeling oddly detached from my body. "*Don't you?*" he screamed. I looked directly at him, or my eyes did. It seemed as if I was sitting on the tundra on the opposite bank, watching.

"I don't know what you mean." My voice stayed monotone of its own accord.

"You always have to say things; you always have to have the last word. I'm just like Dad! You just don't want to admit it!"

"I don't know what you're talking about, I'm sorry," I said. "My dad would never have talked to anyone like this." Immediately I regretted my response. This was not a rational conversation. This was not a rational person.

"*See?*" he yelled. He turned suddenly and looked across the gravel bar. Sally was walking slowly about fifty feet away, her eyes on the ground. "*Just* like *that!*"

He wheeled back around and leaned toward me, his face an inch from mine. "I should *kill* you," he hissed. His words, barbed with profanity, coiled and lashed.

I sat silently. The raft was firm beneath me. It occurred to me that I might die on this river too. It seemed as likely as any other outcome. And just as quickly came the thought that it would be okay if I died here, now. I had been to this place. I had brought the Eucharist to Dad and Kathy's beach. I had glimpsed the truth that this life is mystery. Next to that, death seemed very much a secondary thing.

Another thought: Ned might have just enough sanity to refrain, simply to avoid prosecution. That seemed even more likely.

"I should drown you in this river!" he yelled, suddenly reenergized. Whipping around, he looked downriver. I breathed deeply and slowly. Ned turned back to me.

"I shouldn't have said those things," he said. "I shouldn't have called you those names." The tenor of his voice modulated only slightly, the agitation in his face and body still coiled like a spring.

I sat still and found freedom in the depth of my breathing. I saw time and events and life flowing by on the surface of the river. I breathed. I stayed in the current, then rose high above and looked down at three tiny creatures around a blue raft on a rocky beach in a vast country.

"Let's go," he yelled violently across the gravel bar.

Sally started walking back.

"I'll tell you what you're going to do," he said suddenly, regaining strength in profanity. "You're going to get off this raft and start walking. You're going to walk all the way back to Kaktovik."

I spoke in low tones, and slowly. The sense of calm I felt seemed to have come as a part of the wind, or the water beneath the raft. It was nothing less than grace. "We're all going to get in the raft, and we're going to go to the pickup point," I said. "Let's get in, and let's go."

Sally pushed the raft off, and Ned shoved it hard and leapt in. He sat motionless holding his paddle on his lap, staring downriver.

We were in the main channel, and the river meandered slowly back and forth between gravel bar and banks. The raft pointed itself, requiring only tiny corrections. Our trip returned to silence — or at least to as much silence as there is in the presence of a running river, crying birds, mosquitoes, and all the forms of life in an Arctic summer. The silence in which words and anger might settle stiflingly.

I watched the river flow. Around the raft, and away from me. I knew Sally was right, and recognized a brokenness that I could not and should not try to fix. I recognized it with the same compassionate objectivity I understood the possibility of my death. For the first time, I recognized that the anger I'd just witnessed, now unchecked by my dad's restraint, did not have to be a part of my life.

I saw two people who had known the same person so differently, known life so differently. We were scrawling our own stories across wrinkled pages, and despite sharing relationships and circumstances, our stories bore only a faint resemblance to each other. Each of us staggered forward in different directions with the opportunity — the responsibility — to write our own lives.

I felt shame for the girl I was, the cruelty I was told I had inflicted on Ned as a child. I felt anger. Why had affection seemed a limited commodity in our family? Dad had controlled Ned's outbursts in the past. Why had he not done something to help correct them, to heal the hurts? Why had our family refused to acknowledge and address abusive behavior? I could see, dimly, that the missing acknowledgment also sprang from pain, pain carried from the scars of previous generations.

At the same time, I understood that compassion might exist without connection. I was strong enough to draw those boundaries. Whatever else Dad had or had not done, he had taught me that I was strong enough to create my own life. Each of us had to take responsibility for who we were, and how we reacted to the stones and boulders in our way.

Several years later, looking back at Ned and myself on that raft through the prism of time, I see in Ned the violence of pain in a soul ill-equipped to handle it. I feel a greater sadness than I knew to feel then.

Then, I simply watched the water. The current curling toward the shore, cutting across to the next bend in the river. It parted around rocks, poured over rocks, a transparent force, sometimes glistening, sometimes dark, carrying earth, carrying dreams. I had no control over any part of this, other than how I responded. To death, to anger, to sadness, to joy. That is what the water taught me. I had the right and the responsibility to release abuse from my life. I could not fix the pain. I could not change the anger. This was an unexpected new sadness, a new loss of relationship. But I could choose gratitude over grief. I could choose joy over pain. I could choose healing over abuse. Perhaps for the first time, perhaps prompted by greater losses, I could let go.

◣

In the silence we kept during the rest of the day, I sat on the back of the raft with the current. All you can do to work through the twisted channels of grief is to use the experiences of your life like tools, seeing what might be effective in straightening a board, pounding a nail, aligning the railing of a new reality. And so sitting on that raft moving down the end of that Arctic river, I recalled a Eurail trip in college on which I'd spent three days in Rome, and one day in the red-roofed city of Florence. At the time, I'd planned to double-major in English and art history and, like any good student, had studied Italian art. My love of art had begun long before, rapidly developing beyond the Alaskan artifacts of our local museum. I read about Leonardo in junior high school and started writing all of my journals backward, as he had done, which was easier to do as a left-handed writer. I read everything I could about Bernini in ninth grade.

In Rome, I beelined to Bernini's *Ecstasy of St. Theresa*, tucked away in the tiny Cornaro Chapel. I was surprised by how small the sculpture was; its power for me in photographs had been monumental. Bernini uses a hidden window above the sculpture, allowing natural light to indicate the entrance of the divine, represented by an angel looking down on St. Theresa in a pose of exquisite pain or pleasure. The natural light is enhanced by gilded beams of light behind the statue, further concentrating the understanding of divinity.

But the artwork I remember most had not been one of my favorites from class; the plates in an art history book could not begin to do it justice. And I had to view it through encumbrances protecting a renovation of the Brancacci Chapel in Florence. The piece was *Baptism of the Neophytes* by Masaccio. This fresco, created using a medium of water and paint rendered on a wet surface and relying on the artist's skill in using the fleeting moments before evaporation, was delicate and damaged. From its delicacy emanated a power and a profundity that were only enhanced by its fragility. A neophyte, wearing only a cloth around his waist, kneels in a river, supposed to be the Appelline Arno. St. Peter, shaking in his participation in the sacrament, pours water over the man's bowed head. In water, in light, the entrance of the divine.

Water as the basis of life. Seventy-one percent of the earth is covered by water. A baby's body is born seventy-eight percent water, that percentage falling to fifty-five to sixty as the baby grows to adulthood. Even as adults, our lungs are ninety percent water, our blood eighty percent, our brains seventy percent. In this Arctic desert, water formed the basis of the earth, frozen in permafrost. It created patterns and monuments, surging into cracks to freeze and create polygons, pushing up mounds called pingos, coursing down rivers, moving mountains.

"Over water the Holy Spirit moved." In the Greek lexicon, *photismos*, an ancient word for baptism, means "the act of enlightenment, illumination" or "a bright light." In this enlightenment was mystery. I saw the light on the water, but was only beginning to see the light around me. The coastal plain extended in all directions. When I paid attention, seeing things at just the right angle, the walls I'd built over a lifetime deliquesced in the purity of true wilderness and endless light. The river's rubato lengthened these fleeting moments of wide-eyed wonder into the beginnings of a new reality. I could not create this. I could only accept it as gift, and hope I could learn to see it. The acceptance was the particular slant, the perspective I needed to learn to see. With it, a ray of light cut through the darkness as in a Caravaggio painting, illuminating the beautiful.

In the Requiem, we pray and beg for mercy, clutching at known structures and histories of faith while struggling to find meaning and reassurance in gutting realities. Or rather, that is what the text of the Requiem does — wrestling with darkness to find hope. Praying the Requiem, we are in the mouth of the beast, in the flames of woe, in endless darkness entreating deliverance. That there are words at all which suggest something other than this terror is our only hope. The music allows us to pray words that, at the time, are rocks on the edge of a chasm. Our bodies dangle from the edge, threatening at any moment to fall, to careen wildly against sharp boulders in a descent to the terrible blackness. We claw desperately at the lip of the abyss, clinging to the rocks, even as they crumble. The music is what catches us just as we think we must let go.

In the course of Mozart's illness as he composed the Requiem, he wrote to his father, "Death, when we consider it closely, is the true goal of our existence.... I thank my God for graciously granting me the opportunity ... of learning that death is the key which unlocks the door to our true happiness.... I never lie down at night without reflecting that I may not live to see another day." It is the kind of note one could only write knowing of impending death.

Dad had written in his journal what he learned through death, as well: "Family deaths — a stillborn child, a father, a marriage. I think I have learned a lot from these deaths as I struggle in coping with the aching that such loss brings." And from living through Dad's death, I know that these thoughts must have led him to consider his own death as well.

I felt the raft underneath me, moving easily in the narrow current. Occasionally the scrape of gravel beneath the raft pulled me from my thoughts. I moved the paddle to steer almost unconsciously. Birds flew over us — jaegers, terns, ducks, in ones, then in pairs.

The river branched again. Getting out to pull the raft was tiring, and yet finding the right path seemed impossible. If we'd been able to view the river from above, as we had on the flight in, we'd have been able to see the strands of the river weaving gently in and out; we'd have been able to choose the best route. From river level, the path was not as clear. But I was starting to believe that somehow it all made sense. Somehow there were patterns here to show a way.

I've looked since then at ways to find new slants, new rays of light on dark paths.

I wanted to be angry that this had happened, this attack of a bear, this strange thing, this terrible offense, this attack of nature on my life and my heart. I wanted to say, "My God! I don't deserve this!" But deserving had nothing whatsoever to do with it. I was not unique. I was not alone. This is the human condition, this pain, this loss, and even this violence. Around the world, people lost whole families and friends every day to war, disease, starvation, or circumstance. This pain — and the search for meaning in its wake — is what it is to be human. Realizing this did not assuage my pain, but it did tell me that I was not alone.

Out of the expanse of tundra, river, and sky, sea ice loomed ahead. It was not physically there; it did not actually occur for another couple of miles, and yet there it was. Rays of light bent and inflected, and the mirage of ice shimmered beyond us. It was very real, and yet it was not at all real. More real at least than the refractory lens of memory, more real than the lens of life. The mirage shivered in the air of high latitude, shaking in unseen currents of air. Perhaps the ice was not where I saw it. But I did see it. The laws of physics explained that I saw it. But it was not where I looked. And yet I felt the chilled air blowing over its surface, cooling my skin.

I coveted the mirage. I coveted the seeing, the feeling, even the blurred edges, when all I could see was inky darkness, blinding light, or, worse, nothingness. Not blackness. Not light. Just nothing. Nowhere on earth — or in the soul — is there nothingness. But there is nothingness in the frozen fear of forgetting, the coveting of hard grief, the first kind, the most painful kind, the kind that says that you are alive, and the people now gone were real and are real if only in memory and in some other kind of time than that in which we live each day.

So to see through nothingness, I focused. I focused on the details around the void. I focused on the far horizon and the mirage. I focused on nearby flowers. Slowly, the real of the world, the real of the soul, emerged as substance, taste, and texture, something complex and fresh and sweet, and nothingness faded away.

We came to the pickup point—a day early. There was a day— a whole day—to sit on the tundra and wait.

CHAPTER 16

AN INTENTIONAL DESIGN

No one ... can doubt for long that the path ahead, seen from a tall enough height, will form at least a compelling figure, a clear intentional design, of use to others.

—Reynolds Price, *A Whole New Life*

I sat alone on the tundra. Gear selected to help me stay overnight if weather came in lay around me partly packed: a small tent, food in a bear canister, and the shotgun, loaded. The buzz of the Cessna, shuttling Ned, Sally, and the bulk of our gear, had been swallowed by the breeze the moment the wheels left the tundra. The wind off the polar ice to my north blew gently across the flat coastal plain to my tiny camp. I listened for the low hum I had read about in various Arctic accounts, but heard only the quiet sweep of wind, birdsong, and the buzz of mosquitoes.

A caribou appeared just east of me, stopping to stare with wide brown eyes for a long minute. Like the caribou early in our trip, he simply materialized, a momentary visitation, manufactured by Arctic air. Every part of him, from flank to felt-covered antler, quivered with alertness. He stood for only a minute before trotting off, seeming to dissolve back into the air.

The plain was far from the barren stretches I had imagined I saw during the flight in. In the past year—and the past week on the river — what had been merely a backdrop, an abstract concept of wildness, revealed itself. The land breathed. The wilderness gave, and it took away. It could wound, and it could heal. I had not before understood its complexities. Its loneliness mirrored my loneliness, and invited mine in to sit, and to be, and to understand. To wait and to witness.

Were their last moments blessedly short? Seconds of terror, as I surmised? Or terrible and prolonged? What mattered was that they were gone. No, what mattered was that they had lived. What mattered was that I still lived, even for a moment. What mattered was what I made of this moment.

I looked across the expanse of plain to the mountains beyond, my gaze resting along the gentle contours. I wondered if the low hum I'd heard described was instead the understanding of an intricately choreographed natural dance, too fine to see, too complex to comprehend. The epic land, aerial, and marine migrations to this remote wilderness to birth young, sometimes to die, to continue the cycle, flowed with the rhythms of life itself. There was death, and rebirth. Instead of an end to my journey, a linear picture of progress, each time I looked for conclusion, I came back to circles, loops, cycles. Despite myself, I felt the wind as restorative, life-giving. And I began to accept that this was not betrayal, that this recognition of life in the face of death was the point. This acceptance was how I would honor them. This was how I would live.

I got up to stretch my legs, to do something. But there was nothing left to be done, nowhere to go.

This acceptance I was beginning to feel, like the movement of air from a wing, had something to do with surrender. It had something to do with endurance. It had something to do with faith. The line between the living and the dead may not be much of a line at all, but the terrain is not for the weak of heart. It is treacherous going.

Dad, I've got a concert next month if you want to come. Dad?

I sat back down on the tundra. I watched the line of the river-bank for a long time. Recognizing mystery brought peace, even if it still eluded my understanding. Staying true to that hope and my faith was the map. Endurance. Tenacity. "I continue to notice how much success has to do with staying the course," Dad had written. "You just have to keep on keepin' on," said my grandma.

I would not see Ned again after this, except for very occasional meetings at a family wedding, a family funeral. I learned on this river to set a boundary against abuse, whatever its cause, in spite of its sadness. I learned about the corrosive acidity of anger. I learned to love through separation and separateness. Learning to be strong, from my dad, from a river, was about choosing beauty in a world of pain.

"I can only encourage you to live your own life," wrote Dad.

But I don't know how. I don't know if I can do it well, if I can make you proud, Dad. There was so much I didn't understand. Quarrt-siluni, say the Inuit. Sing of beauty. Wait. Witness.

What I had seen only a week before, a barrenness in the simplicity of quiet lines of landscape, now pulsed with life and possibility, a living heartbeat, wild and fragile. We were separate. We were the same. I felt a physical thrill, like an electric current through my body. I was learning to see. I had seen: in landscape and light. I was learning to hear. I had heard: in the breeze, in music, in worship, in silence. The prickly toughness of tiny tundra plants crunched under me as I shifted to sit cross-legged, eyes, ears, and heart open to a different world.

Ninety-five percent of plant life in the Arctic is below the surface of the earth. Only five percent is visible. If I couldn't see it in myself, I could see this regeneration in the Arctic. It had, and will always have, a lot to teach me. I see so little. So much of what I know of Dad, of Kathy — so much of what I know of myself, and this world and the world to come — is hidden. Any discovery will always be only the beginning of knowledge. Mystery reigns. Without the extensive and unseen root and rhizome systems of Arctic vegetation, the tiny plants and flowers would die. What is known might sometimes sustain us, but what is unknown will save us.

This is what I learned then and realized later. That it was not about finishing a trip. It was only about living in the midst of what cannot be understood. Learning to see. Learning to hear. Bearing witness. Trusting that what is hidden is beautiful.

A constant overflight of jaegers and songbirds moved through the Arctic air, their cries and songs coming and going in crescendos and decrescendos along lines of breeze, written on a score of fog at the ocean shore, the patterns of tundra polygons, mountains rising to the south. The animals that made this place their home: the elusive musk ox, the fox upriver, the wolves who had perhaps watched me, even if I had not seen them. The bears keeping a respectful distance — grizzly bear, polar bear, black bear. A hundred thousand caribou following mysterious rhythms along ancient migratory paths. The Arctic not only pulsed with the world's heartbeat; it was the heart. And with it all — under, above, and around it all — flowed the river. I breathed slowly, deeply, and the tundra seemed to breathe too, and our breath was one breath, our heartbeat one heartbeat. For this short time, I belonged.

Dies irae ... I walk through the valley of the shadow of death. I walk through the valley. I walk through. Through. The valley ends. The mountains become holy hills, and the valley opens to the plain. In Adam all die, but all shall be made alive. *Dies irae ... lux aeterna.*

Even under cloudy skies, the light lay warm and comfortable across the plain. The kind of light that dissolves shadow, dissolves bristling tooth and claw. The kind of light that shows the transparency of things. Once, in a choir, I'd sung Herbert Howell's Requiem singing words by John Donne: "Bring us, O Lord God, at our last awakening," we sang, "into the house and gate of heaven ... no noise, no silence, but one perfect music, no darkness nor dazzling, but one perfect light." On the other side of a symphony, on the other side of a scream, is silence, the one perfect music. On the other side of darkness, on the other side of shadow, is one perfect light. In witness is worship. Worship despite tragedy. Worship because of tragedy. A Kaddish.

I wondered then — and I have wondered many times since — why I haven't had the same kind of dream with Dad as I had with Kathy. I am certain, as certain as I am of gravity and air, that Kathy and I were together when I had that dream. But Dad hasn't come to me the same way. I've wondered about this for years with a sense of dread and sadness. But I have come to believe that he was always with me. That whatever was unsaid or unresolved was never there to begin with, dissolved instantly in that kind of love only a parent knows for a child. I know this looking at my own children. And this is something that was hidden to me then, that kind of love. For anyone who has experienced it, how do we not walk around awed by hope that so much love can exist in one physical place?

Dad, I don't know what else to do. It feels like there should be more. This is all I can figure out. This is the best I have.

Shannon, it is enough. You are enough. I love you, kiddo. Live your life.

I unzipped my fleece to feel the wind against my skin. My time here was short; *chronos* time imposed itself without mercy on the river time of the last week. I had come to honor my father, to honor Kathy, to mourn, to grieve, to acknowledge that place where they had left this world. Or that is how I'd defined it, a thin mask for going to the ends of the earth to try to find them. To see if there was a way to bring them back. But in coming to honor them, I had begun to learn from this place that honoring a life is honoring the wide open space of wilderness and unknowing where the sacred dwells.

In Dad's journals, he had mused, "No one could draw a picture of this place and what it has meant to me, but when I think of Alaska

I think of sun and light and earth and trees. Although it's entirely different ... the outdoors reminds me of my youth in Kansas. There as a 10-year-old we wandered through endless fields ... floating small streams." Alaska gave him life and took it away. But after leaving home to travel so far, it was in Alaska, in a land of lines and light, that Dad finally was able to come home.

If the response to pain is beauty, beauty must win. I don't think I could have articulated this back then. But I had needed to do something. I had needed to do something beautiful. In that beauty was hope. In that hope was healing. Even if it took a lifetime. To wait and watch is to witness. To witness is to see the sacred in the massacred.

I wish you could have been at the concert in February, Dad. We sang Mozart's Requiem. I sang it for you.

I was there, Shannon. I always am.

The drone of the Cessna arrived a moment before the plane appeared, a tiny spot swelling imminently, crudely interrupting the rhythms of wilderness, the timelessness in which I sat suspended. Tundra air blew over the river and the wind felt to me like sadness. I had finished Dad and Kathy's trip. This part of my journey had ended. I had done what needed to be done. I had put one foot in front of the other, dipped the oar back into the water. Grief would weave itself among the strands of love and life and hope, and I was starting to believe that what came of it all would still one day be beautiful.

Do not be afraid, says the angel. Don't be afraid, said Sam Fathers. Looking out over the tundra, I was still scared. But I was no longer afraid.

Requiem aeternam. Grant them rest eternal. Perhaps it is not for the dead that we should pray; they rest eternally already. Perhaps it is our own poor souls that need these prayers.

Λ

Back in Seattle, just off the shore of Lake Washington, two eagles fly together, their flight twisting and turning, circling and coiling, ascending higher and higher, an exquisitely intimate and primal dance. One flies underneath the other, its back to the lake as they soar into the sky, higher and higher. Their talons clasp and they fall, hurtling toward earth, the flat plane of the lake, and then they break off, each pair of wings snatching the air, pulling their bodies back into the slipstream, and they fly out of sight.

EPILOGUE

It is the mountains again, always the mountains. The sky is blue, a blue that makes me imagine anything is possible, and it sets off the white-and-blue hanging glaciers of Mount Shuksan against dark greenschist rock. I stand next to Dad's army friend George, waiting, laughing nervously, more nervous each minute. A few close friends are clustered around me, each in a knee-length, cranberry-colored silk dress of her own choosing, the warm sun drawing strong shadows under collarbones and cheeks. My dress is white, a simple lean design made of raw silk with a champagne-colored sash hanging to the ground in back below a row of tiny covered buttons.

The details are in place. I hadn't worried too much about them, and things had arranged themselves in all the right ways. Two small bouquets of flowers have been placed on chairs in honor of Dad and Kathy, and a special note to them included in the bulletin. There is a picture of them at the lodge where we will hold the reception. We are standing in the perfect mountain meadow. There is a band that will play "Brown Eyed Girl." I'd splurged on flowers. I wonder if I should be thinking more of them, but it is a momentary wonder. I am where I am supposed to be, waiting to walk to the person with whom I will spend the rest of my life, without whom I can't imagine spending another day.

"It will just be a few minutes, I think," someone tells me.

I know we have arrived on time and am not worried, but the delay seems to stretch like a lazy cat well after sunrise.

"What is it?" I ask.

"They're just trying to get people seated," a second person says. But the delay is longer than something like that would require.

"Seems like it's taking a while," I say to break the awkward pause, to calm my own nerves.

The two who've been talking glance at each other; something uneasy passes between them. Then there's a pause.

"There's a bear that's come into the meadow," someone says gently. "It's not a problem. He's just eating grass, but we're trying to get him to move. He's right in the path where you girls are about to walk."

The sky flashes blue. The glacier winks. The spruce trees are suddenly the deepest green.

"A bear," I say quietly. "With all those people in the meadow. Wow."

I look at George, and we both smile small easy smiles. I think I see George's eyes glistening. Of course there is a bear.

"It's okay," someone says, quickly. "We're trying to get him to move along. He just doesn't seem to be in a hurry."

It is a half hour later when we finally walk down the hill toward the meadow, the girls in their silk dresses and the guys in tuxedos, and finally George holding his arm firmly under mine. I walk down the small hill, where there is no longer any evidence of bear, and toward the meadow, and up between the chairs, where I had thought I would feel self-conscious, but I look at my husband-to-be ahead of me, the man who will be the father of our children, of Dad and Kathy's grandchildren. I see Peter's smile and the tears in his eyes. And a world and a life that are deep and complex and full of wonder.

AFTERWORD

This story took place in 2006. In 2007, the Arctic lost more sea ice than ever in recorded history, and the trend continues.

The wild coastal plain of the Arctic National Wildlife Refuge remains threatened by development, despite its fragility and criticality as breeding grounds for large numbers of animals from air, land, and sea, ever-decreasing estimates of oil, and a deteriorating pipeline system putting at risk not only the transport of oil but national security. I traveled to the Arctic mourning a loss as open as this wilderness, my family crushed under the weight of a bear's nature; this unforgiving landscape is as susceptible to human actions.

The killing nature comes from instinct. Human threat is born of premeditation. There was no way to stop the deaths of my dad and Kathy. There is a way to prevent the destruction of the Arctic. While climate change continues to loom as the Arctic's biggest threat, the immediate threat of widespread development presses further. Developers claim they need only two thousand acres to develop the Arctic Coastal Plain; they do not explain that those two thousand acres will pepper the plains like a checkerboard, requiring roads and helipads and other destructive infrastructure on tundra perfectly suited for the cruelty of an Arctic winter, and utterly unable to withstand human development.

We are an oil-based society, but there is important work being done to reduce our dependence through conservation and alternative energy sources, and this is where our resources and attention should be given. The Alaska Wilderness League is doing important environmental protection work for our northernmost public lands in Alaska's Arctic. The bipartisan Rocky Mountain Institute is doing important work to develop alternative energy and conservation-based solutions for our country. Conservation is our way out. Conservation is the only responsible path, for the sake of the environment, our national security, our way of life, and creation itself.

Five percent of author revenue from *North of Hope* will go to support the work of the Alaska Wilderness League.

NOTES

1. Daniel Merkur, *Powers Which We Do Not Know* (Moscow, Ida.: Univ. of Idaho Press, 1991).

2. Ibid.

3. J. Gelineau, SJ, "Music and Singing in the Liturgy," in *The Study of Liturgy*, ed. Cheslyn Jones, Geoffrey Wainwright, Edward Yarnold, SJ, and Paul Bradshaw (New York: Oxford Univ. Press, 1992), 498.

4. Brian Payton, *The Shadow of the Bear* (New York: Bloomsbury, 2006).

5. Paul Shepard, *The Sacred Paw* (New York: Penguin, 1985).

6. Doug Peacock and Andrea Peacock, *The Essential Grizzly* (Guilford, Conn.: Lyons, 2006), 44, 46.

7. Peter Kivy, *The Fine Art of Repetition: Essays in the Philosophy of Music* (New York: Press Syndicate of the Univ. of Cambridge, 1993), 26.

8. Ibid., 27.

9. Gerald G. May, *The Wisdom of Wilderness: Experiencing the Healing Power of Nature* (New York: HarperCollins, 2006), 30–34.

10. John Haines, *The Stars, the Snow, the Fire* (Minneapolis: Graywolf, 2000), 52.

11. Mary Oliver, "Bear," *Why I Wake Early* (Boston: Beacon, 2004), 41.

12. Beryl Markham, *West with the Night* (New York: North Point, 1942), 62–63.

Shannon Huffman Polson lives and writes in the Pacific Northwest. Her writing has appeared in a number of literary magazines and periodicals, as well as two anthologies. Polson graduated with a BA in English Literature from Duke University, an MBA from the Tuck School at Dartmouth, and an MFA from Seattle Pacific University. She served eight years as an attack helicopter pilot in the army and worked five years in corporate marketing and management roles before turning to writing full time. Polson serves on the board of the Alaska Wilderness League and sings with the critically acclaimed Seattle Pro Musica. She has looked for adventure and challenge anywhere she can find it, scuba diving, sky diving, and climbing around the world, including ascents of Denali and Kilimanjaro, and completing two Ironman triathlons. She and her family enjoy backpacking, any kind of skiing, paddling, and spending as much time outdoors as they can in the western states and Alaska. In September 2009, Polson was awarded the Trailblazer Woman of Valor award from Washington State Senator Maria Cantwell.

Polson can be found at *www.aborderlife.com*.